Contents

THE LAKES

THE COAST

WATERSIDE WALKS
in the
LAKE DISTRICT

Colin Shelbourn

To PG

Published by Sigma Leisure – an imprint of
Sigma Press, 5 Alton Road, Wilmslow, Cheshire SK9 5DY, England.

British Library Cataloguing in Publication Data
A CIP record for this book is available from the British Library.

ISBN: 1-85058-805-8

Typesetting and Design by: Sigma Press, Wilmslow, Cheshire.

Cover photographs, top to bottom, left to right: Tarn Hows; Rydal Water; Crummock Water; Mill Beck, Buttermere; Elterwater; Aira Force; Stanley Ghyll; The Upper Esk; Derwentwater; Loweswater; Thirlmere; Leverswater and Church Beck; sunset over Arnside *(All photographs by Bill Stainton)*

Maps: © Colin Shelbourn 1998, 2004. Maps based on original research compiled locally by the author. Map of walk locations based on the Lake District Lap Map published by Cardtoon Publications Ltd.

Printed by: Interprint Ltd, Malta

Disclaimer: the information in this book is given in good faith and is believed to be correct at the time of publication. No responsibility is accepted by either the author or publisher for errors or omissions, or for any loss or injury howsoever caused. Only you can judge your own fitness, competence and experience. Do not rely solely on sketch maps for navigation: we strongly recommend the use of appropriate Ordnance Survey (or equivalent) maps.

INTRODUCTION

There are far too many mountain summits in the Lake District. I will rephrase that: If you are a keen walker, it is far too easy to be lured by the mountain summits. You dig out the OS map, think to yourself, "Hmm, I've only climbed Scafell Pike 437 times but it's a while since I did it from Wasdale", and before you know it, the sandwiches are made, the rucksack is packed and you are heading for the hills. Even worse, you might become a peak bagger, ticking off the summits like a hyperactive trainspotter.

If this description strikes a chord, it is time to calm down and discover a secret. In addition to all the brown bits with the exciting contour lines, the Lake District also features significant amounts of blue. Within the boundary of the National Park, there are 16 lakes, over 400 tarns and innumerable rivers, streams and waterfalls. They are all rich in wildlife, features and interest, each with a unique mood and atmosphere, yet too often regarded as distractions to the serious business of climbing the high fells.

Waterside Walks in the Lake District seeks to redress this balance. By concentrating exclusively on routes that are along, around and, in some cases, *through* water, you will discover a whole new perspective on Lakeland. The beauty of this approach is that the walks are so varied. This book covers everything from a simple, 1km stroll to a 9km hike into the mountains (I couldn't keep out of them entirely), from exhilarating waterfalls to tranquil, isolated mountain tarns. It means there is something to suit a wide range of tastes and abilities, from families with small children to hardy types who fancy a day off from the high fells.

The 25 walks are arranged by type and in length order, shortest first. This broadly matches how much energy you will expend doing them. With the exception of the first, all the routes are circular, Ullswater and Derwent Water including a boat ride. The final walk, across Morecambe Bay, is unusual as it is outside the National Park, is offshore and doesn't get a route description. This is because it can only be done as an organised walk with the official guide. However, it is a unique experience and had to be included. The description gives full details of when and how to join the walk.

Each route follows the direction that gives the best views (in my opinion), defaulting, wherever possible, to follow the flow of rivers

1

and becks. There is something curiously satisfying about this but I haven't been too obsessive about it. I'm not keen on books that break up the route descriptions with great wodges of history or anecdotes, so I've kept these to the end of each walk, with a note on the map so that you won't miss any features of interest.

The three appendices give additional information, which I hope will enhance your walking in the area. I've rounded up the remaining lakes and given a brief mention to a few extra favourite routes in Appendix 1. Appendices 2 and 3 give public transport and general tourist information about the area.

Bear in mind when doing these walks that many waterside habitats are fragile environments. Do not go scrambling into tarns and rivers if it means causing erosion or damaging the plant life. If you are tempted to swim, bear in mind that the water can be freezing cold. The lakes, in particular, remain cold throughout the year. Some of the lakes and tarns are plagued with blue-green algae in summer. This is unpleasant for humans but dangerous for dogs and children. If the water looks unclear, or you see warning notices, keep out.

On the subject of warnings, choose your footwear with care. Some of the walks get boggy in winter but I have no idea how anyone stays upright in wellies on wet rock. For the longer routes, and the walks into the mountains, you will find proper walking boots much more comfortable. If you want information on boot hire or where you can hire baby buggies or backpacks contact one of the tourist information centres listed in Appendix 3.

If you are unfamiliar with the Lake District, you will notice a few unusual phrases cropping up. 'Beck' is the local word for stream, 'force' is a waterfall and 'ghyll' (or gill) is a wooded valley, usually containing a stream. Many of these terms come from the Norse settlers, who probably also originated the following Lakeland question: How many lakes are there in the Lake District? One – Bassenthwaite Lake; all the others are waters or meres.

Throughout the walks, I was ably assisted by my chief researcher, Manchester, who also happens to be my dog. His contribution was invaluable. He showed me which paths to avoid when he rushed ahead and created a lot of splashing noises.

Finally, there are far too many Lakeland rivers and tarns for one book. If you get hooked, regard this as a starting point. Open a copy of the OS Outdoor Leisure maps, select a speck of blue, find a right of way to it and go exploring. You'll rarely be disappointed.

TARNS, RIVERS AND WATERFALLS

Stanley Ghyll *(Bill Stainton)*

1

SPOUT FORCE

Spout Force is a waterfall for connoisseurs. It is not very famous or dramatic but it is hidden in the hills, just off the Whinlatter Pass, and easy to overlook as you speed past in the car. It is an easy stroll to reach it and there is a super viewpoint overlooking the waterfall.

Distance and terrain: 1km (0.6 miles). An extremely easy walk with a short climb at the end.

Parking: There is very limited parking (three cars) in the quarry lay-by at Scawgill Bridge, 3.5km (2.2 miles) west of the Whinlatter Visitor Centre on the B5292 road between Braithwaite and Lorton (GR 177257). Alternatively, use the Forest Enterprise car park, just off the B5292 at GR 182256 (approximately 0.5km east of Scawgill Bridge).

If you have chosen the Forest Enterprise car park, you have two choices; either walk down the road to the Scawgill Bridge start, or follow the signs for Spout Force and follow the way-marked route across the fields and down the side of the gorge. A longer, way-marked trail will eventually bring you back to the car park; I don't recommend retracing your route to the car park as the pull up through the conifer forest is only for the extremely fit.

Starting from the Scawgill Bridge lay-by, look for the public footpath sign just before the bridge and go through the kissing gate. A path leads along the stone wall, just above the fast-flowing Aiken Beck.

When you come to the next gate, take a moment to examine the amazing stone wall on your left. It consists of small slates, piled horizontally to climb the steep hillside. A very impressive example of the stone-waller's art.

Continue along the path, the river bordered by a larch wood on

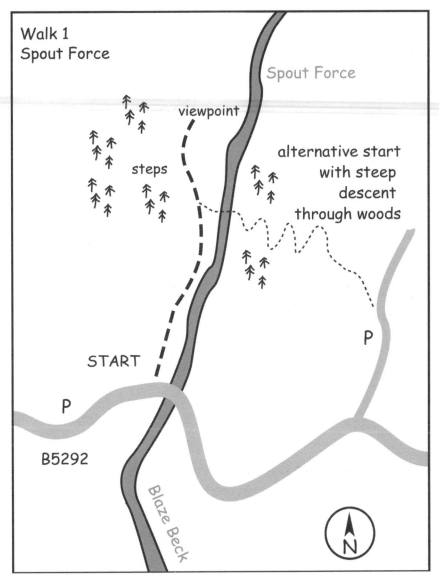

Walk 1
Spout Force

Spout Force

viewpoint

alternative start
with steep
descent
through woods

steps

P

START

P

B5292

Blaze Beck

N

your left and a dark conifer wood on the right. The sides of the river valley rise very steeply. Look out for buzzards circling overhead (they have a cry not unlike a seagull).

You pass a wooden footbridge, where the path from the upper car park emerges from the trees. Continue following the river upstream and a set of steps leads you into the larch wood. After a short climb up the side of the hill, the path leads out to a fenced viewpoint and a surprise. A few metres in front of you, Spout Force [1] gushes out of a deep cut in the hillside.

To make the complete circuit, retrace your steps a few metres and the path continues into the wood, climbing the hill on your right. This is the way-marked forest trail. Our route consists simply of following the outgoing path back to Scawgill Bridge.

NOTES

[1]   Spout Force is a 7m (25ft) cascade in a sheltered cleft in the river valley. Popular with climbers keen to practice their ice techniques when it freezes in winter.

2

THE HOWK, CALDBECK

This is an easy walk which takes you through one of north Cumbria's prettiest villages. The unusually named Howk is a waterfall that dashes through a picturesque limestone gorge, hidden in the woods on the western fringe of the village. Caldbeck has two recently restored mill buildings, with the opportunity to pay 10p and see a waterwheel in action.

Distance and terrain: 2km (1.2 miles). Very easy terrain but some muddy sections in wet weather.

Parking: National Park Authority car park just off the B5299, Caldbeck to road (GR 323399), signed 'Caldbeck Conservation Area'.

Walk towards the far end of the car park, past the level, green areas, and turn up the little tarmac lane to the T-junction and the duck pond. Turn left and follow the lane to another T-junction, opposite Bridge End stables. Go straight across (look for the slate sign on the barn wall: 'Footpath to the Howk'), through the stable yard and out again along the track on the far side.

Whelpo Beck is across the field on your left. After 30m, you pass through a kissing gate and the wooded side of the gorge starts to rise up around you. Glancing back to the village, notice the tall chimney stack amongst the houses. This is an old brew stack [1]. You pass a couple of small weirs and then come to the first of two mill buildings [2].

Continue past the mill, squeezing between the building and the wall of the ravine. You are walking upstream, past a series of small cascades and after 50m or so come to a flight of stone steps. Up the first dozen or so and suddenly you have a view of the Howk.

The waterfall cuts through the limestone, forming a bowl, just below you. It is sheltered by the rock and the surrounding trees, forming a very pretty view, especially in spring. Continue up the

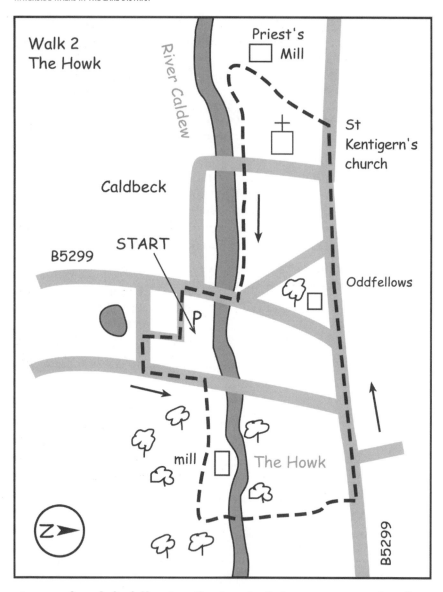

Walk 2
The Howk

Priest's
Mill

River Caldew

St
Kentigern's
church

Caldbeck

B5299

START

P

Oddfellows

mill

The Howk

B5299

steps and go left, following the handrail down to a wooden foot-bridge. The path splits at this point. Straight ahead, the path goes to another, smaller waterfall (worth diverting to) and then heads out across the fields to Whelpo. Our route goes left, over the footbridge, and gives another opportunity to view the Howk.

Once over the bridge and up another flight of steps, you leave the woods via a kissing gate and head straight across the field to another kissing gate. Look for the farm building and the four tall pines ahead of you; the gate is just to the right. Crossing the field is very tranquil after the noise and drama of the Howk and you get a good view to High Pike and the Caldbeck Fells in the distance. (But not, unfortunately, to the second-best-named fell, Great Cockup, which lies just behind the Caldbeck hills. For the best-named fell, see the Crummock Water walk.)

When you leave the field, you are on the B5299, so dogs on leads. It is not a busy road but there is always the chance of meeting a young farmer on a souped-up tractor.

Turn left and follow the road back into the village. You go past the junction of roads, with the map shop and walnut tree on the triangle in the middle. Continue through the village [3] and as you cross another beck, look out for the clog maker's shop on the right.

After ten minutes, you pass St Kentigern's church on your left. Cross over and go down the lane just past the church, signed 'Priests Mill' [4].

St Kentigern's most famous resident is John Peel, the huntsman and subject of the song, 'Dye ken John Peel'. He died in 1854 and his grave is in the churchyard, on the left.

The lane leads you to Priests Mill car park. At the bottom, turn left and follow the churchyard wall to a small bridge over Cald Beck. Just past the bridge, look out for St Kentigern's Well, a small trough on the river bank. Then, without crossing the bridge, continue along the narrow path, past the Rectory, to the road. Turn right, over two bridges, and you are back at the entrance to the car park.

NOTES

[1] The seventeenth-century building was probably once a fulling mill, used for processing sheep wool. During the nineteenth century, it became a brewery and in 1829 there were six pubs in the village.

[2] The first of the two buildings at the Howk is a timber drying store where wood was stored for up to a year to get rid of moisture before it was made into bobbins. The bobbin mill was built in 1857 and at one time employed 60 men and boys. It had a water wheel almost 13m (42ft) in diameter, the largest in the country. Alas, the wheel no

longer exists, having been taken away and scrapped during the second world war. The mill closed in 1920.

[3] Caldbeck village gets its name from the Norse description of the stream, 'kaldr beck' or cold stream. It originally developed as a rural settlement until lead, copper and coal were discovered in the surrounding fells. During the eighteenth century, the village became a centre for rural industry with mills springing up along the river to spin wool, grind corn, and make paper and bobbins.

[4] Priests Mill was built in 1702 by the rector of St Kentigern's. It was originally a corn mill, power coming from a 4m (14ft) diameter water wheel. The mill was sold by the church in 1901 and continued working – first as a corn mill and then a sawmill. It was still working as a joiner's workshop until 1967, when it fell into disuse. Restoration work began on the mill in 1985.

The earliest part of St Kentigern's church is a Norman archway, dating back to 1112. An earlier, wooden church probably once stood on this spot. The present building is mostly late medieval though a great deal of restoration was done in 1880. St Kentigern (sometimes known as St Mungo) was the sixth-century Bishop of Glasgow. Just behind the church is a road known as Friar Row; the name comes from a hospice that was maintained here in medieval times by the Prior of Carlisle.

3

STOCKGHYLL

Harriet Martineau, the diarist and close friend of Wordsworth, said of Stockghyll: "It is the fashion to speak lightly of this waterfall, it being within half a mile of the inn, and so easily reached; but it is, in our opinion, a very remarkable fall (from the symmetry of its parts) and one of the most graceful that can be seen." Once you've done this walk, you will agree that Stockghyll is a hidden treasure a superb waterfall within fifteen minutes walk of the centre of Ambleside, ideal for families with young children or anyone who wants to escape the shops and traffic for an hour.

Distance & terrain: 2km (1.25 miles). The path is good in dry weather but can be muddy in winter and is steep in places. A stretch of potentially slippery rock to negotiate on the way down.

Parking: Several good car parks in Ambleside but the best is the South Lakeland District Council car park on Rydal Road (the A591 from Ambleside to Grasmere). Entrance opposite Charlotte Mason college. The walk starts from this car park.

L eave the car park via the footbridge and turn right along the pavement. The peculiar small stone house on your right is known as the Bridge House [1] and is built over Stock Beck. The other building to note is the Glass House, an innovative glass workshop, gallery and restaurant run by Adrian Sankey. Just over the road bridge, cross to Bridge Street, the small alley or 'ginnel' on the opposite side of the road (it's directly opposite Dodd's Restaurant and signed 'Footpath to North Road, Old Bark Mill'). Once known by the more picturesque name Rattle Gill, this cobbled alley leads you between some of the oldest houses in Ambleside. You pass under the first storey of one of the houses, then emerge by the river, alongside the old waterwheel.

Turn right at the road and into the middle of Ambleside. Note the market cross on your right as you come to the main road, then go left, past the Salutation Hotel and go up another alley between Barclays Bank and the old Market Hall [2].

This brings you to a lane called Cheapside. Turn left (signed 'To the Waterfalls') and continue uphill. This is a quiet lane, without much traffic, which runs alongside Stock Beck. The building on the far bank was once a mill, briefly became a holiday complex and is now largely holiday homes.

After five minutes or so, just past the entrance to Stock Ghyll Croft, turn left, off the road and into Stock Ghyll Park. The path takes you through a wood and alongside the river. Look out for the old dam, just as you pass the first of the park benches.

Once past another bench and a set of wooden steps, the path forks. Go left, down steps to a wooden footbridge, which acts as a collecting point for branches washed down the river at times of high rain. As you cross, you can see the tree-lined river gorge opening up ahead of you. The path climbs steeply above the level of the river. The sides of the gorge are full of mosses, plants and a sprinkling of trees. If you keep to the metal fence, it will lead you to a good view of the waterfall and the pools.

Retrace your steps to the path and continue up to the wooden bridge at the top of Stockghyll Force. Once over, continue right. Careful as you go past the wooden picnic table and cross a rock outcrop, which gets very slippery when wet. Just past the next bench there is another picnic table and the path forks. The path down is across the new access path to the right, but it is worth walking left for 100m or so to have a look at the wonderful Victorian turnstile, the upper entrance to the park [3].

Return to the path and continue downhill. Once again, look out for viewpoints thoughtfully provided by the Victorians. The first of these occurs just past the set of concrete steps. Double around the tree and there is an excellent view of the waterfall. The second one occurs a few hundred yards further on the metal fence stops in the tree trunk.

Continuing downhill, you pass a small house on the left and then join the outgoing path. Retrace your route into Ambleside and try one of the many cafés for a tea.

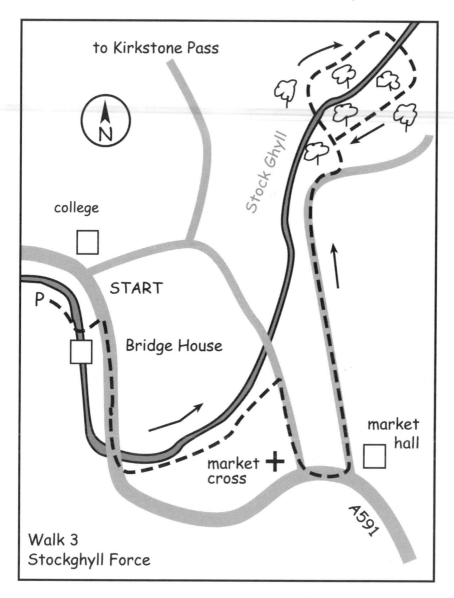

to Kirkstone Pass

N

college

START

P

Stock Ghyll

Bridge House

market
cross

market
hall

A591

Walk 3
Stockghyll Force

NOTES

[1] The Bridge House has a long and varied history. Built sometime
between 1650 and 1700, it has been a weaver's shop, a cobbler's, an
antique shop and a tea room. Incredibly, it was also once a family

home and six children were raised here. They must have been very small and well behaved; the main room is less than 4m by 2m. There is a hoary old legend that it was constructed by a canny Scotsman to avoid Land Tax but in fact it was originally the apple store belonging to Ambleside Hall, when this part of town was an orchard. Ambleside Hall used to stand on the corner of North Road and Smithy Row and the Bridge House is now a National Trust shop and information centre.

Stock Ghyll once powered three woollen mills in addition to corn, linen, and paper and saw mills.

[2] Ambleside received its market charter in 1650 and it is from that date that the present town developed. Prior to that, the medieval village had grown along North Road, on the packhorse route up Kirkstone Pass.

[3] The 18m (60ft) drop of Stockghyll Force was a popular visitor attraction in Victorian times. They built the bridges and iron railings and installed the gate at the top. Visitors were charged 3d (about a penny) to see the waterfall.

4

AIRA FORCE

Aira Force is Lakeland's best-known waterfall and is heavily promoted as such by the National Trust, which owns the surrounding land. This means that in summer you could be queuing up to the use the car park and the path to the falls will be engulfed by coach parties. It is worth the effort to go early in the day or late in the afternoon; when you can get it to yourself, the waterfall is magical.

Distance & terrain: 2km (1.25 miles). Very easy walking to Aira Force, ideal for families and junior walkers. A few tree roots and rocks to scramble over to reach the upper bridge.

Parking: National Trust pay-and-display car park at the junction of the A592, Glenridding to Pooley Bridge, and the A5091 to Dockray. There is also a free car park less than a mile along the A5091. From this car park, you walk across the field to join the walk from the upper bridge.

A t the back of the National Trust car park is a slate canopy and an information point. Go through the archway alongside and follow the path through the shady pine woods. Once through the second gate, you can see the river on the right. Through a wooden gate and between two yew trees and you come to a footbridge. Once across, the path splits two ways, beside another large yew tree. This is a pleasant open area [1] and a strong indicator of the days when this was all part of Gowbarrow Park.

Go straight ahead and follow the wooden fence to the gap and the steps down to the footbridge over Aira Beck. Once you've crossed, disregard the path that goes left, along the bank, and go up the steps to climb above the river. The path splits again 40m further on, just below a massive Scots pine. Although this is taking you away from the river, go right and the path climbs to give you a view of Ullswater

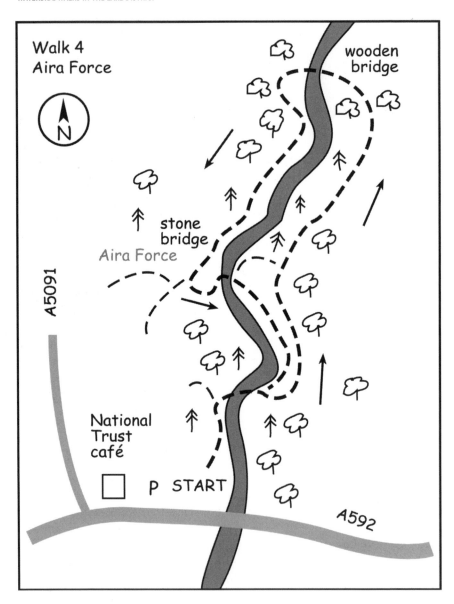

Walk 4
Aira Force

N

wooden
bridge

stone
bridge

Aira Force

A5091

National
Trust
café

P START

A592

and Place Fell. Keep inside the fence (don't cross the stile where the path forks) and just past a park bench, the path forks again. Go left again, downhill, towards the sound of the river in the wooded ravine ahead.

Aira Force, Ullswater *(Bill Stainton)*

You pass a rock outcrop and come to the stone bridge over the upper falls. This is a good viewpoint but don't cross it for now. Instead, go right, following the river upstream and ignoring the steps off to the right, 20m past the bridge. This is a lovely, wooded walk, climbing past a series of small cascades, with plenty of places to dabble hot paws.

The path is rougher and narrower but keeps to the river throughout. There is a bit of scrambling over rocks and tree roots. It comes to an apparent stop on a ledge, overlooking a gorge and a long cascade. The rock has been cut away by the water and the trees overhang the ravine to form a very cool, picturesque spot. As an added bonus, few of the crowds who come to see Aira Force bother to explore this far so you may be lucky and get it to yourself.

Just before the ledge there is a path to the right. Go up and bear left, to continue upstream. After 10m, go left and you can see a wooden bridge ahead. After another 20m, the path zigzags right to join another path. Go left and shortly afterwards left again.

You're climbing above the ravine now but heading upstream once more. After another 50m, the path forks again. Go left and down to the wooden bridge. It stands over a very narrow gully, which is very dark and mossy. Notice the rowan, emerging from the side of the gully at a right angle.

Once over the bridge, go straight, following a wire fence for 25m before heading downhill again. Don't be tempted by the erosion path lower down, by the river bank. The upper path is rocky in places.

You eventually drop to the level of the river and back to the upper bridge. Don't cross but go right, up a few steps and then the path descends once more. It takes you into a clearing, to a bench seat and a view of Helvellyn.

The path splits here. Take the left fork and down 103 steps to the classic view of Aira Force. Make use of the handrail as the slate steps can get very slippery. As you carefully descend the steps, you can feel the temperature drop and the air freshen.

The steps bring you down to the lower bridge. From this position, you are looking straight up the waterfall to the upper bridge [2]. After a heavy thaw you will need to wear waterproofs to stand here for long.

Continue over the bridge and the path heads downhill. Ignore the steps coming in from the left after 30m or so (this way round the walk is designed to minimise climbing steps!). The path winds its way along the side of the wooded ravine. Tall pines tower above, giving the feel of a vaulted, cathedral roof.

The path drops down towards the level of the river and arrives back at the first wooden bridge. Go back over the bridge and retrace your steps to the start of the walk.

NOTES

[1]   It was along this part of the shores of Ullswater that William Wordsworth spotted a host of golden daffodils. Although he later claimed to be wandering lonely as a cloud, he and his sister Dorothy, were walking together to visit their friend Thomas Clarkson, the anti-slave trade campaigner who lived at Eusemere (near Pooley Bridge). Dorothy's diary for April 15, 1802 reads: "I never saw daffodils so beautiful, they grew among the mossy stones about and about them, some resting their heads upon these stones as a pillow for weariness and the rest tossed and reeled and danced and seemed as if they verily laughed with the wind that blew upon them over the lake, they looked so gay, ever-glancing ever-changing." These notes later became the inspiration for William's famous poem.

[2] Aira Force is a spectacular sight. A 21m (70ft) cascade cuts
through the rocks and crashes into a deep pool. Ten years ago, when
writing about this fall, I commented that the sound of water is
drowned by the click of shutters. Today I should add the whirr of
motor drives and the flash of automatic cameras. It has been a
popular spot for centuries. Wordsworth described it in 1835 in his
Guide to the English Lakes as: a powerful brook which dashes among
rocks through a deep glen, hung on every side with a rich and happy
intermixture of native wood.

5

MILL BECK, BUTTERMERE

Driven by the desire to circle the lake, most visitors to Buttermere village overlook this little walk. They are missing out. This is a short stroll which follows Mill Beck to Crummock Water and then heads upstream into a dark gorge, to a fascinating series of cascades above Buttermere village.

Distance and terrain: 2.75km (1.75 miles) including the 0.5km digression to Crummock Water shore. An easy stroll down to the river followed by a not too strenuous climb to the waterfall. Good grip is recommended in the wet as the waterfall section can get muddy and slippery.

Parking: National Trust pay-and-display car park on the B5289, just outside Buttermere village, on the Crummock Water side. Much easier to find a space than in the car park in the centre of the village.

L eave the car park via the kissing gate on the north side and join the main path from the road, turning left and heading into Long How wood. The path leads down through the trees to Mill Beck, a delightful river which flows from below Newlands Hause to Crummock Water.

The path runs right along the river bank, below an outcrop of rock. The path has been extensively worked by the National Trust so, as you might expect, it is level and dead easy to follow. You get glimpses across the fields to Red Pike and Sour Milk Gill. The other two becks, cascading down the fell at the head of Crummock are the imaginatively names Far and Near Ruddy Beck. Ill let you guess which is which.

As you reach the footbridge, there is a tantalising glimpse of Crummock Water ahead. Cross the bridge and over the stile, into the field. The route goes left (signed 'Buttermere Village & Scale Bridge

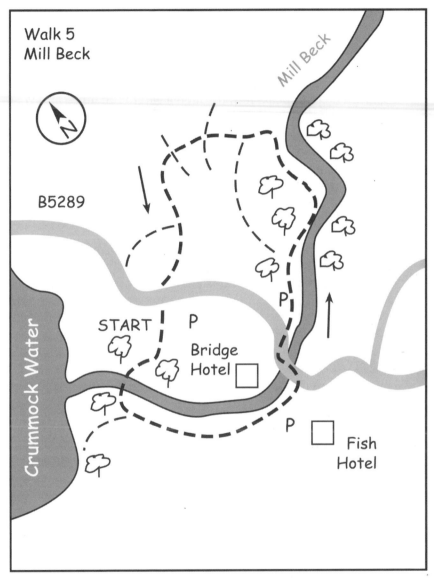

Walk 5
Mill Beck

Mill Beck

B5289

START

P

Bridge
Hotel

P

Fish
Hotel

Crummock Water

& Force') but take a diversion right and follow the path along the river and into Nether How wood. This brings you to a pebbly beach at the southern end of Crummock and a magnificent view along the lake to Mellbreak and Grasmoor. If you haven't already done it, the Crummock Water walk follows the far western shore below

Mellbreak and climbs up behind the mountain on the left, over the saddle between Mellbreak and Gale Fell.

Back to the river and stile and head towards Buttermere village. You're walking alongside the river, beneath trees and gradually you come into view of Fleetwith Pike and Haystacks, at the far end of Buttermere. The path bears left, through a gap in the fence and goes between the river and the field boundary, spurning the footbridge to Syke Farm.

The path brings you into the National Park car park. Walk up through the car park, past the toilet block and cafe, averting your eyes from the picturesque holiday apartments behind the Bridge Hotel. You come out on the road beside the Bridge Hotel. Turn left and, immediately over the road bridge, turn right and enter Ghyll Wood to rejoin Mill Beck [1].

A clear path through the wood now takes you through delightful woodland, climbing alongside the river gorge. At the confluence of the two rivers, there is a small waterfall. Look out for the ferns covering the rocks and thriving in the dark, damp atmosphere.

Another 100m uphill and the path forks. Left does a gradual climb to the top of the wood but if you are feeling fit, go right, which has the best views. This drops down to the river side and winds along the side of the gorge, giving you the opportunity to enjoy the vigorous torrent as it plunges between the rocks. Look out for the weird and wacky oak tree, growing over the river and covered in ferns and moss.

At the footbridge, turn left for a steep, thigh-burning pull to the top of the wood. The easier path comes in from the left. If any of the party have taken that route, they'll be feeling less exhausted but you can feel more smug you've had the best views.

There is an unusual ladder stile, complete with integral gate, which takes you out of the trees, onto open fell side. Now you have a choice: turning left takes you down alongside the wall and fence line and back to the road, opposite the car park where you started. It is the easier of the two routes and you get good views of Buttermere but they are not the best.

For those, you should go straight up through the bracken, keeping to the distinct path, straight over at the next two crossroads of paths. From the second crossing you start to descend. Divert to stand on top the outcrop on your left and you gain a brilliant view of Buttermere.

Rejoining the path, keep going down, heading towards a large, rocky knoll on your right. Where the path splits, go right, winding below the crag, alongside a bog. As you approach the fence line, a small beck runs alongside the path.

The path swings left, around the crag and runs downhill, beside the field boundary, to emerge on the road, opposite the main entrance to Long How wood. Go through the gate and turn left, back to the car park and starting point.

NOTES

[1]   The river is called Mill Beck because it fed the corn mill which once stood on the site now occupied by the Bridge Hotel.

6

FINSTHWAITE TARN

This is a two-part walk; after you have explored the reservoir there is the opportunity to visit the bobbin mill it was built to power. In recent years, the area around the tarn has been developed and improved by the National Park Authority and is now a serious rival to the National Trust's Tarn Hows. In my opinion, Finsthwaite is the better of the two – quieter, more mysterious and far more of an adventure to discover.

Distance and terrain: 2.75km (1.75 miles), excluding the walk to Stott Park Bobbin Mill. A climb to High Dam then a mostly level walk around the tarn. Can be muddy in places.

Parking: If visiting the Stott Park Bobbin Mill, park at their car park and use the off-road footpath to High Dam. Or use the small, free car park, below High Dam. (On the Lakeside to Finsthwaite road, signed 'Finsthwaite, Rusland and Satterthwaite', coming from Lakeside, the turning is the first on the right, past the village sign for Finsthwaite.)

The car park for High Dam is tucked in the trees at the top of a narrow tarmac lane. There is no passing traffic, so the walk begins immediately you've got your boots on and let all dogs, children and assorted relatives out of the car. Head uphill into the woods, away from the lane. You're accompanied by a strong beck, which comes crashing over the rocks on your left. Although narrow, the beck has several short cascades that are worth looking out for.

The track leads to a farm gate and kissing gate. On the other side, the route forks. The track goes right but you should follow the path straight ahead.

After a 100m or so, ignore the footbridge over the beck and continue up the stony path. You are walking through heavily coppiced woodland [1] of birch and oak. Continue climbing through

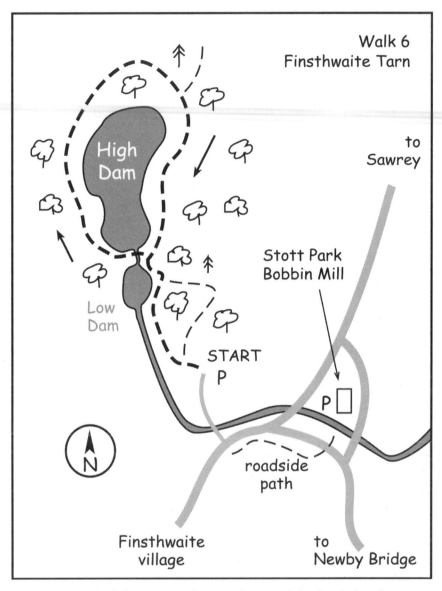

Walk 6
Finsthwaite Tarn

High
Dam

to
Sawrey

Low
Dam

Stott Park
Bobbin Mill

START
P

P

N

roadside
path

Finsthwaite
village

to
Newby Bridge

the trees, with the constant hiss and roar of the beck. At the stone wall, go through a second kissing gate and keep straight ahead (ignore the path off to the right). After another 200m, you enter a band of fir trees and come to the first dam. This stands at the foot of a small, pretty reservoir, surrounded by fir trees. This is Low Dam and

25

there is a path across the dam and around the other side. However, as it can be very muddy and difficult to follow, resist the temptation and continue uphill. After crossing two footbridges, you come to High Dam [2].

At the wall, turn left and cross the dam. Look out for the valve for the outflow pipe, in the water on your right. This was installed when a turbine was used to power the bobbin mill at Stott Park, replacing an earlier waterwheel.

The wall is about 100m long. At the end, you plunge into the trees, a dense larch wood. The woods provide a thick, overhead canopy but the trees themselves are not too closely planted, giving plenty of room for other vegetation to thrive.

The path is easy to follow. The simple rule is where it branches off, stick to the shore. The path winds along the shore, past the island and then crosses a beck and goes through a stone wall. The path forks, left signed to Rusland. Go straight, along the clearer path and after 50m you begin to climb away from the tarn and up the side of Great Green Hows. Reaching a wire fence, bear right along the fence, parallel to the low ridge on your left.

After five minutes of steady walking, you can glimpse the tarn again. Arriving at a wooden seat, you get a lovely view across the tarn to Gummer's How in the distance.

The path drops downhill and over another beck. After another 50m you reach the wide, open marsh at the head of the tarn. The path here is very clear. At one time, you walked across via a series of wooden board walks but latterly the National Park has built a neat cinder path, underlain with plastic matting. It keeps the path clear of mud and gives it a curiously spongy feel as you march across.

Cross the marsh, past gorse and heather and then you are back into the woods. This is mixed woodland for a short spell and then you encounter larch again. Ignore the path off to the right, which heads to the stone wall, and continuing winding round to the tarn, which comes back into view after 100m or so.

The final part of the walk is a delightful stroll along the bank, winding through mixed woodland, with constant views over the water. Look out for the bench by the water, a brilliant spot for a picnic.

Eventually the path brings you back to the dam wall and you can retrace your steps to the car. Note that below the top kissing gate there is a broad track that goes off to the left; this will take you down to the lower gate, avoiding the steeper parts of the path.

Once back at the car, it is worth making the short walk to Stott Park Bobbin Mill, which was, after all, the whole purpose for the tarn being developed. Walk down the lane to the main road and turn left. After 50m there is a path on the far side of the road, signed 'Permitted Footpath to Stott Park Bobbin Mill'. Follow this path and it brings you opposite the car park entrance to the mill [3].

NOTES

[1] Coppicing was the practice of cutting back birch, oak and ash saplings to provide the raw material for charcoal burning. The area around Rusland and Backbarrow supported a number of mills and furnaces and the surrounding woods are heavily coppiced. Birch was also used for making the bobbins and reels which supplied the thriving nineteenth century, Lancashire cotton industry. A large mill could make use of around a million bobbins a week.

Demonstrations of charcoal burning can sometimes be seen at Brantwood, John Ruskin's home at Coniston. Contact Coniston tourist information centre for details.

[2] High and Low Dam were developed in 1835 from the original Finsthwaite Tarn, to provide power for the waterwheel at Stott Park Mill.

High Dam is smaller than Tarn Hows but, in my opinion, more interesting. It is much less cultivated and, surrounded by larch woods, it has a dark, mysterious air. It is easy to feel very isolated here.

[3] Stott Park Mill was built in 1835 by John Harrison, a gentleman farmer, originally to supply bobbin reels to the cotton industry. It was one of the Lake Districts most important mills and continued producing bobbins until it closed in 1971. English Heritage bought the site and reopened it as a museum in 1983. The two original curators used to work in the industry (though not at Stott Park) and were able to give wonderful guided tours and demonstrations. The mill is located as close as possible to its raw materials, in this case water power from Finsthwaite Tarn and birch from the local woodland.

7

LANTY'S TARN

Lanty's Tarn is a brilliant little reservoir hidden in the hills above Glenridding. It is surrounded by trees and easily missed in the mad rush to get to the top of Helvellyn. Whilst the vigorous, hardy types toil up the mountain to tick off another summit, you can do this walk and enjoy some unusual views of Ullswater, then gently meander back alongside Miresbeck and Glenridding Beck.

Distance and terrain: 3.5km (2 miles). A steep climb to the tarn up an excellent footpath, then an easy descent along Miresbeck.

Parking: National Park Authority car park in the village centre (follow signs for tourist information centre). Pay and display.

The car park has one or two interesting points. Look around and you will spot a footpath sign pointing to the far corner, which bears the single, laconic word 'Helvellyn' [1].

Walking back to the entrance, you pass the National Park tourist information centre, which has a mining cart on display outside. There is a larger display about Greenside Mines [2] inside the centre.

Leave the car park via the main entrance, go right to cross the road bridge and turn right immediately before the grocery store (signed 'Public Bridleway: Mires Beck, Helvellyn'). How many other local grocers do you know who hire mountain boots? Turning up the narrow lane alongside Glenridding Beck, you pass an outdoor store, a couple of houses and Glenridding public hall. Continue past the kennels and along the track through Eagle Farm.

200m past the barns, the track forks. You will be coming back along the right-hand track (unless you get hopelessly lost) so take the left fork (signed 'Lanty's Tarn, Helvellyn'). You begin to get a good view right into Greenside and along the valley to the old mine workings.

Pass 'The Croft', an attractive Lakeland stone terrace, and the path forks. You can go either way but if you go left, through the narrow gate and past the garden, you cross a footbridge and come out alongside a small waterfall in the trees. Go right – passing the alternative gate – and follow the path up the hillside.

The path is a bit rough here but you quickly get onto the maintained section. As you climb the field, you get a good view back across the valley to Glenridding Dodd and Sheffield Pike. You go up alongside a wire fence and as the path goes left around the fence, stop at the wooden bench seat and take in the view of Ullswater – a small hint of what is to come.

Climb to a kissing gate and once through, the path leads you right, across open fell side (signed 'Lanty's Tarn, Grisedale & Striding Edge'). You now have a very good view into the valley below. Turn round slightly and you can take in Ullswater and Place Fell.

The path leads to a stone wall and forks again. Go left, continuing uphill and enjoying better and better views. At the top of the field, you get a real panorama; Ullswater and Place Fell, around to Gowbarrow Park and Ulph's Tower and further left to Glenridding Dodd and Sheffield Pike. The path drops to a kissing gate in a stone wall, but before going through, it is worth a 15-minute diversion left to climb the pine covered knoll. From here you get a 360-degree view of the surrounding fells. You can look down into Grisedale, left to Place Fell and on to Ullswater, appreciating the distinct bend in the shape of the lake.

Walk back to the kissing gate, go through and you arrive at Lanty's Tarn [3]. Walk to the end of the tarn (ignoring the path that goes right, at the end of the fence) and you come to the concrete dam wall. A clear track goes down from this into Grisedale, but look right and level with the wall you will spot a narrower path, heading up the side of the small hill on your right. Take this path and you climb away from the tarn, towards Dollywagon Pike and Helvellyn. Look left and you can see into the valley, up to St Sunday Crag and, a little further left, glimpse the straight ridge of High Street, between the peaks in the distance.

The path takes you around the little grassy knoll onto open fell, heading towards a group of conifers. You can go straight on to the conifers or you can bear right across the slightly boggy field. Either way, you are heading towards the stone wall and gate you can see on the skyline to your right,

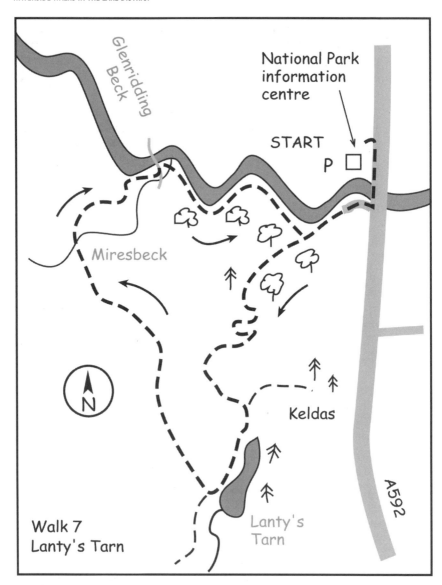

National Park
information
centre

START

P

Glenridding Beck

Miresbeck

N

Keldas

A592

Walk 7
Lanty's Tarn

Lanty's
Tarn

At the gate there is another terrific view. High Street and Place Fell on your right, Ullswater and then the flat top of Glenridding Dodd, with Sheffield Pike and Raise to the left.

Go through the gate, heading towards Swart Beck, the white streak on the fell to the left of Sheffield Pike. Crossing a couple of minor becks, you head around the fell side along an easy path, which follows the contour of the hill. Round the end of the fell, over two larger becks and you begin dropping towards a stone wall and a deciduous wood. The crag rising in front of you is the Nab, part of Birkhouse Moor.

Once at the wall, keep going straight and you begin to hear the rush of water. You come to the end of the wall and reach Miresbeck. Cross the beck and turn right, over another beck and heading downhill, in the direction of Glenridding and Ullswater. You drop down to a farm gate and ladder stile and once through you are on a rough vehicle track, heading downhill through the field.

The track drops to an isolated cottage. Turn left, following the track to another set of gates and a T-junction. Left is signed 'Greenside Mines', but you go right, continuing down the track to cross the river and join a tarmac lane. Left along the lane to a crossroads. On your left is a very neat caravan park. Go right (signed 'Path to Car Park') and cross Miresbeck for the last time. This takes you down a track between a camping site and Glenridding Beck [4]. As you walk along the bank, notice the reinforcements on the far side. This is a very pleasant part of the walk, which takes you along the tree-lined river bank and brings you back to the outgoing path. Turn left and walk back into Glenridding.

NOTES

[1] This is a regular starting point for the climb of one of the big four Lakeland mountains. At 950m (3118ft) high, it is probably the most rewarding of the major peaks and it attracts walkers like a magnet. Unfortunately not all of them realise what they are letting themselves in for; on one memorable occasion in late Autumn, I encountered a gentleman on Striding Edge in jeans, carrying a collapsible umbrella in his rucksack.

On that particular day, the peak was covered in thick mist and a National Park ranger, a friend of mine, was stationed on the summit to advise people how to get back down. We stood together in the grey cloud, watching walkers advance out of the murk, and chatted about the weather and mortgages. It didn't seem in the least eccentric at the time.

Visit the National Park information centre in the car park, and you will find a fascinating relief model of the Helvellyn range.

[2] Greenside Mine was established in the seventeenth century to mine lead and silver. In fact, the history of mining in this area probably goes back to Roman times. The mine was very productive throughout the eighteenth and nineteenth centuries: In 1875 it produced lead and silver worth over £1 million, proving to be one of the most profitable in England. Ore was carried by packhorse to Keswick or Alston Moor and then, with the coming of the railways, to Newcastle. The mine pioneered the use of electric locomotives and electric winders to work the shafts. Mining ended in 1962, although local enthusiasts still explore the levels and set off occasional test explosions. You can find more information about the mines in an excellent display in the Glenridding tourist information centre.

[3] Lanty's Tarn was once entirely natural. Its name is a contraction of Lancelot's Tarn, after Lancelot Dobson, the last man to own the tarn before it became a reservoir. He sold it in the 1820s to the Marshall family, the owners of Patterdale Hall (which is now the Patterdale Youth Hostel). They dammed the outflow and used the tarn for fishing in summer and for making ice in winter. The tarn is around 2m (6.5ft) deep.

This is a lovely spot. The tarn is flanked by conifer plantations and there are birch trees along the edge of the water. It is very quiet here, no sound of rushing water, just the occasional bleat of a solitary sheep and, in my case, the sound of the chief researcher digging up the landscape.

[4] Glenridding Beck is a spectacular torrent after a thaw and the embankments are vital in spring. The most dramatic flooding came after a night of heavy rainfall on 30th October 1927. The dam at Kepple Cove burst, sending a quarter of a million gallons of water and 25,000 tons of rock and debris crashing into the valley. Many homes were washed away but incredibly no one was hurt, although there were newspaper reports of dramatic and heroic rescues. The debris from the flood spilled out into the lake and formed the promontory that now serves as the car park at the Ullswater steamer pier.

8

TARN HOWS

A classic walk in one of the most popular spots in the Lake District. Tarn Hows is owned by the National Trust and the footpath around the tarn was refurbished in 1993 to provide a gentle, level stroll. Ideal for older and younger legs and for those in between who want a pleasant, undemanding walk. For the more adventurous, the route starts with a climb alongside Tom Gill. Those feeling less energetic can use the National Trust car park at Tarn Hows.

Distance and terrain: 4km (2.5 miles). Apart from the moderate climb alongside Tom Gill, it is all very easy, level walking.

Parking: Limited free parking off the road at Tom Gill, 400m south of Yew Tree Tarn on the A593 (GR 323998). If cheating, use the National Trust pay-and-display car park at Tarn Hows.

Looking north from the car park, the path goes straight into the trees beside the road, over a footbridge and then bears right to start climbing. Dogs immediately off the lead, what could be better?

The path climbs alongside Tom Gill. There are occasional paths into the woods, mostly diversions. The river bends left and you can see a stone wall and field on the opposite bank. A path comes in from the right but keep to the river side to another fork. Go right, climbing alongside a narrow ravine and past a small waterfall. Note that at the end of a long summer, this is a raging torrent of damp moss.

Continue along the river to a kissing gate in a wire fence. Through the gate and upstream to join the main path at Tarn Hows. Turn left and follow the yellow brick road around the tarn [1].

The path forks after 200m. Keep right, following the path around the head of the tarn. The route is very easy to follow and little description is required from me. When in doubt, bear right and keep close to the tarn. At the head of the tarn, the path veers away through a very wide kissing gate, then leads you back into the trees.

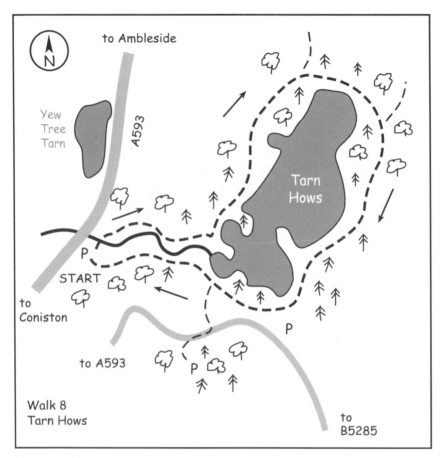

to Ambleside

N

Yew
Tree
Tarn

A593

Tarn
Hows

START

P

P

to
Coniston

to A593

P

Walk 8
Tarn Hows

to
B5285

Shortly after the kissing gate, there is a path off left, through the stone wall, which goes across the moor to Arnside Intake. This is a pleasant diversion and considerably quieter. No one ever goes to Arnside Intake so if you want somewhere quiet to eat your sandwiches, this is a diversion worth taking. After visiting the little tarn, retrace your steps and continue along the main path around Tarn Hows.

As you begin to approach the road again, you pass through a second large kissing gate and the path forks. Keep bearing right, staying as close to the water as you can, rather than going up to the road. This brings you back to the main gate, by the dam at Tom Gill.

Do not go through the gate but instead turn left. There are two paths in front of you; the wide path goes to the car park, the narrower, right-hand path climbs to a fallen tree trunk and a view of

Tarn Hows with Wetherlam in the background *(Bill Stainton)*

the tarn. Turn right along the trunk and the route heads off down a narrow path, away from the tarn and down through bracken. A stone wall and the woods will be on your right.

As you drop down alongside the wall, you can see the path up through the woods on your right. The wall turns into a wire fence, then drops to a derelict stone barn. Turn right and then, where the path forks, go straight alongside an old wall and down to a wooden farm gate. Go through the gate and turn right, down an unmade vehicle track. This takes you straight back to the car park and the start of the walk.

NOTES

[1] This area originally consisted of a number of smaller tarns, called Monk Coniston Tarns. In the 1850s, the outflow was dammed by James Marshall of Monk Coniston Farm, to make a larger tarn and provide power for a local saw mill. Tarn Hows has been in the possession of the National Trust since 1930 and a survey conducted in 1974 estimated that around 750,000 people visit the tarn each year. However, it also revealed that only ten percent of them actually walk round the tarn. That's still an average of over 200 a day so the only time you are likely to get the place to yourself is in the depths of winter. Say around three o'clock in the morning.

9

STANLEY FORCE AND RIVER ESK

Stanley Force is not the Lake District's longest waterfall but its setting in a deep, wooded gorge makes it one of the most picturesque and dramatic. This is a short walk which combines the falls with a stroll along the Esk, a strong candidate for the title of Cumbria's prettiest river.

Distance and terrain: 4.2km (2.5 miles). A level walk to the first of the bridges over Stanley Ghyll, thereafter progressively steeper with some potentially slippery rock. The short section above the final bridge is optional and should be tackled with caution in wet weather. The walk back along the Esk is level and easy.

Parking: National Park car park at Trough House (GR 172003). Driving west from Hardknott to Ravenglass, it is the first turning left after Dalegarth Station (about 300m beyond the station). This is an isolated car park so ensure all coats, rucksacks and crown jewels are hidden from view.

Go left out of the car park and follow the unmade lane, past the entrance to Dalegarth Hall. You go through a wooden farm gate and past two field gates. This is a crossroads of walks; the left is signed 'Boot and Upper Eskdale', the right 'Eskdale Green'. Continue past the gates (signed 'Stanley Ghyll' and 'Birker Fell') and as the lane curves right, there is a pair of wooden gates in the stone wall on your left. Once through you are into the National Park Stanley Ghyll Access Area (signed 'Waterfalls').

Walk straight ahead and you come to the river. Turn right and follow the river upstream. The riverside footpath is clear and easy to follow and leads you through a mature, mixed woodland. This has been heavily planted in the past and the gorge wall is a mass of thick vegetation, dominated by large rhododendrons.

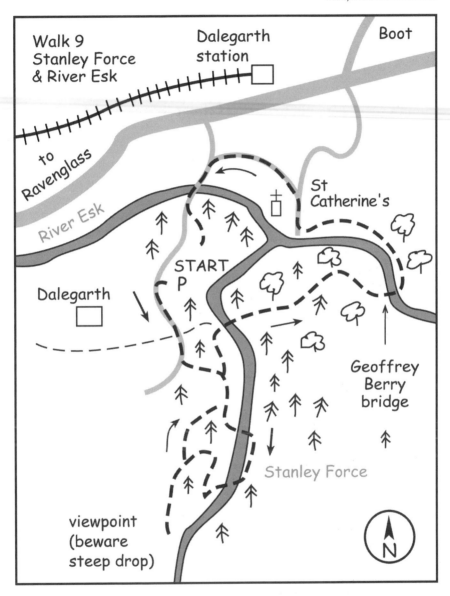

Walk 9
Stanley Force
& River Esk

Dalegarth
station

Boot

to Ravenglass

River Esk

START
P

Dalegarth

St
Catherine's

Geoffrey
Berry
bridge

Stanley Force

viewpoint
(beware
steep drop)

N

After a few hundred metres, the sides of the gorge start to close in.
When you arrive at the first wooden footbridge, you can see the rock
face of the gorge wall ahead of you. The bridge looks as though it
might present exciting possibilities; the far side appears to be

perched on a pile of stones. The setting is such that you may feel compelled to hum the Indiana Jones theme as you cross the bridge.

Continue up the far bank, beginning to climb. The wall above you is thick with ferns and rhododendrons and the rocks are covered in moss. After 80m you come to the second bridge and once across climb a set of steps cut in the rock. At the top of the steps, the path splits. You'll be coming back to this point so, for the time being, head straight, dropping temporarily to the third bridge.

You can now glimpse Stanley Force plummeting between the cleft ahead. The skyline ahead is a narrow v-shape as the sides of the gorge rise above you. The roar of water is loud and the atmosphere tremendously fresh and invigorating.

Half way across the third bridge is a stile and a notice which warns that the path ahead is steep and slippery. In heavy rainfall, the next section of path can be tricky but at other times it is safe enough if taken carefully. Once over the bridge you climb the side of the gorge for a further 50m to a splendid view of Stanley Force [1].

The path ends here; a fence and sign just below this viewpoint makes it clear that this is the limit of public access, however there is an additional view of the waterfall. Retrace your steps to the top of the steps, between the second and third bridge, and follow the hand rails (rather than down to the second bridge). They lead you up the side of the gorge, following a second beck upstream. As the path levels off, there is a slate footbridge over the beck. Cross the beck and go up the hill, past a sign that warns '150ft sheer drop, rock viewing platform 150 yards'.

The path leads a short distance through the trees to a metal fence and the top of the rock crag. Dogs and children on leads as you approach this. From the top of the crag you peer straight down into the gorge for another view of the waterfall. It is a good view but not as spectacular as the view from below, so don't feel you've missed out if you decide to hold back. Incidentally, there is a stile at the end of the metal fence. Crossing into the field, you can work your way over the top of the river to another viewpoint on the opposite side of the gorge you can see it from the rock platform but the view is disappointing. There is so much vegetation that the waterfall is hidden from view.

Retrace your steps to the slate footbridge, then continue straight up the wooded hillside on the other side. The path winds around the hill, on the side away from the gorge, and drops down through the trees towards a stone wall. The path forks, the left going down to a farm gate. Ignore this and go right and the path takes you back to the outgoing route, beside the river.

When you reach the point where you joined the path, at the entrance to the woods, continue along the bank until you come to a wooden footbridge. Cross and leave the woods via a farm gate.

The path goes three ways. Bear left, across the field and the path leads you through the oak trees to the River Esk. This is a very pretty river, the banks overhung by rowan and birch. Turn right along the bank, heading upstream. You pass the stepping

The upper reaches of the River Esk, with Bowfell and Crinkle Crags beyond *(Bill Stainton)*

stones to the church, on the far bank. The stones are usually slippery and often under water, so don't try and cross here. Continue along the bank for a few more minutes and you enter a small gorge and come to a wooden footbridge [2].

You can explore further along the tree-lined bank but this side is a dead end. Cross the gated bridge and walk back along the bank towards the church. Go through a kissing gate and after 100m arrive at St Catherine's church [3].

Turn right to a farm gate and once through, go left, along the track between the stone walls (signed 'Public Bridleway'). This route takes you back alongside the river to the road. At the road, turn left, over the bridge.

The view from the bridge can be entertaining in summer. The river is quite deep here and there are often various noisy characters swinging off ropes and diving into the pools. It's also a favourite spot for scuba enthusiasts on practice dives.

Just across the bridge, you have a choice. You can either follow the road back to the car park, or you can cheat. To do this, look for the narrow gap in the stone wall on your left. This is a variety of stile known locally as fat man's agony. Squeeze through and walk straight up the gentle, wooded hill, back to the car park [4].

NOTES

[1] The ghyll plunges 11m (37ft) into a dark pool, overhung by vegetation. Notice the tree trunk that spans the gorge above the falls.

[2] The bridge was built in 1990 as a memorial to Lakeland writer and photographer, Geoffrey Berry. A dedicated campaigner for Lakeland conservation, Geoffrey was Secretary of the Friends of the Lake District for ten years from 1966. He was Consultant Secretary from 1976 until his death in 1988, at the age of 75. He wrote several books, notably 'A Tale of Two Lakes', which told the story of the Friends' campaign to prevent North West Water and British Nuclear Fuels Limited extracting water from Wast Water and Ennerdale Water. He was awarded the OBE in 1977 in recognition of his conservation work. The Geoffrey Berry Bridge was designed and built by the National Park Authority and National Trust, the £5,000 cost funded entirely from donations.

Geoffrey's photographs appeared in numerous books and in the Victoria and Albert Museum. His pictures illustrated my first book, so I always remember him as I walk this part of the Esk.

Look underneath the bridge and you will see that it is supported by two steel girders, all that remains of the branch line which once carried iron ore from the nearby mine to the Eskdale railway at Boot. Until the bridge was built, walkers crossing the gorge required strong nerves and a good sense of balance.

[3] St Catherine's church dates from the 17th century and is built on the site of an earlier chapel. There is a particularly interesting memorial

to Tommy Dobson in the churchyard. He was the founder and master of the Eskdale and Ennerdale foxhounds and in his day was as famous as Caldbeck's John Peel (of the song, 'D'ye ken John Peel'). He was a bobbin turner by trade and when he died on 2 April 1910, this stone memorial was erected by nearly 300 friends from all parts of the country.

[4] There is a stone packhorse bridge further upstream, called 'Doctor Bridge'. You can extend the walk to include this. The bridge was widened in 1734 so that the local doctor, Edward Tyson, could take his pony and trap across.

10

RIVER GRETA

The River Greta winds its way along a spectacular river gorge, once traversed by the Cockermouth to Penrith railway. Now the railway line is disused and, in an excellent example of creative park management, has been turned into an easy, level walking route. After walking the line, the return is via Brundholme Woods, along the side of the steep river gorge. This is an ideal walk for families and hardy, mountaineering types who fancy a day off.

Distance and terrain: 5.2km (3.25 miles). A very easy walk along the old railway line, most of which is suitable for pushchairs or wheelchairs. The section through Brundholme Woods is hilly, with some narrow and muddy sections.

Parking: Keswick railway station car park (GR 273238). To find it, leave Keswick town centre and head north along the A591. Turn right at Great Crosthwaite church and first right to Briar Rigg. The station is 1km along this minor road. Alternatively, park on the road in Fitz Park, on the southern approach to Keswick, and walk to the station through the grounds of Keswick Spa.

The start of this walk is wonderfully straightforward: stand on the station platform, call out "All Aboard!" and set off down the track [1].

The track continues through the outskirts of Keswick, passing a row of council houses and the sports field and passing under a grey, slate road bridge. The track narrows at this point and you approach the A66 flyover, which spans the river valley via four magnificent arches. As you pass through the two gates, look along the length of the flyover and notice the sweeping curve of the arch. You'll also notice the thump and rumble of lorries passing overhead.

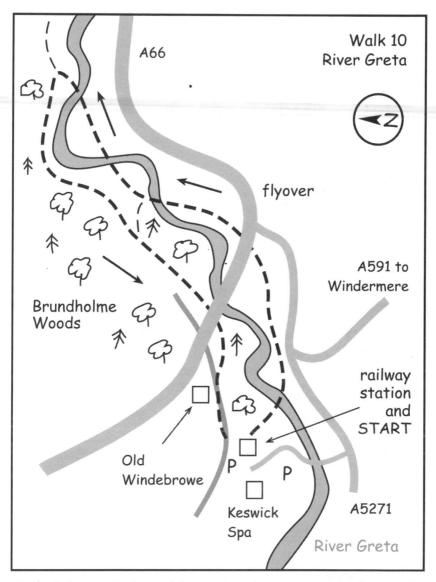

Walk 10
River Greta

A66

flyover

A591 to
Windermere

railway
station
and
START

Brundholme
Woods

Old
Windebrowe

P

P

Keswick
Spa

A5271

River Greta

The path leaves the line of the track at this point, to climb up to the main road. Dogs on leads for this bit. As you reach the road, the path swings downhill again, via a short flight of steps, back towards the river. The conifer-covered fell on the far side of the river valley is Latrigg.

As you descend you get a surprising view of the river, the wide, tree-lined gorge and the weir below. You drop down to rejoin the line of the track and walk upstream alongside the Greta. This must have been a dramatic train ride. The track is nearly 10m above the level of the river giving you an unparalleled view of the 50m wide gorge. You pass under another narrow bridge, into a cutting and arrive at a railway platform. This is Low Briery [2] and there is disabled access here to the track from the nearby caravan site.

Shortly after you emerge from the cutting, the Greta does another loop and the track goes over another magnificent, 80m long bridge. Just on the far side, a set of steps leads into the woods, a way of shortening the walk if necessary.

150m further along the track, the river bends again, so you have to cross over another bridge. The track is several metres above the surrounding woodland and this section of the walk is very pretty.

Just beyond the bridge, look out for the square box on your left. This is an old grit box, used for scattering lime on the track in winter. A few metres on, there is a stile in the wire fence on your left. If you are feeling adventurous, you can cross into the woods and walk along the river bank to the next bridge. There are a couple of benches along the way, the second one marked in memory of Alf Price, from members of the Keswick Anglers Association.

Keeping to the track, you come to the most picturesque of the bridges – a suspended, 40m long structure and the last for this route. The railway line carries on for another 3km to Threlkeld village and you can link it with a walk beside the River Glenderamackin. But for now, turn left after the bridge and cross the stile into the field (signed 'Keswick via Brundholme Woods'). Climb up the steep bank, over another stile and you are into Brundholme Woods.

The path leads downstream along the steep side of the river gorge. You climb 71 log steps and come to a T-junction. Go left (signed 'Keswick'). The path winds its way through the woods, following the contours of the hill, crossing a number of pretty becks and keeping in view of the river throughout. At times, the side of the hill drops away very steeply to the river, some 20m below.

Eventually, the path drops to the level of the river and after 1km or so, you can see the line of the railway track on the far bank. The path leads past a small, dark conifer plantation and brings you back to the A66 flyover. From this bank you get an even better view it. On the far side of the river at this point is a collection of buildings that once housed the local saw mill.

The path ends at a gate and flight of steps. The gate leads you onto a tarmac lane beside a small bridge. The permissive path, however, goes right, up the steps and back up the river bank. Follow the path through the woods and it brings you to Old Windebrowe and the Calvert Trust riding stables [3].

Go through the stable grounds to the minor road and turn left. After 50m you come to a sign pointing left ('Footpath to Keswick'). You could follow the lane back to the railway station car park, but for a more interesting route, go left here, doubling back along the drive to Brundholme Country House. As you come to the house, there is another path off to the right (signed 'Footpath to Keswick'). This leads you into the rhododendron bushes, alongside a field and gives you another good view of Latrigg.

Over a bridge and then the path leads into the grounds of Keswick Bridge timeshare. As you drop down towards the road, you can see the Keswick Hotel on your left. At the road, go left and up the steps to rejoin the railway walk. Turn right and you are back at the station. If anyone says you are late, blame leaves on the track.

NOTES

[1] Rail transport arrived in Keswick in 1864, with the building of the Penrith to Cockermouth railway. Designed to finish the link between the ore fields of the west coast and industry in the north east of England, the line cost £267,000 for just over 50km (31 miles) of track, including 135 bridges. The line followed the present route of the A66, hugging the western shore of Bassenthwaite Lake. It must have been a magnificent line to travel: imagine sitting in a carriage, eating your nineteenth century Supersaver breakfast sandwich and seeing Blencathra and Skiddaw speeding past the window. The Penrith to Cockermouth line closed in June 1972, although the sandwich was last seen in a buffet car on the Glasgow to London train in September 1996.

It's a great shame that the station itself has been allowed to become so derelict. It ought to be a museum, café or information centre, extolling the virtues and history of the surrounding area. Fortunately, the track itself is in excellent condition – a broad, flat, tree-lined route that very quickly brings you to the first of the bridges and a view of the river. As you cross, notice the iron railway girders under the bridge. The steps on the left, on the far side, lead to the Keswick Bridge timeshare development. You will be returning up these steps.

[2] Low Briery is the site of one of the 20 bobbin mills in the Lake District operating in the mid-19th century, a time when the Lake District supplied 50% of world-wide demand from the cotton industry. Low Briery's 40 million bobbins a year were exported as far afield as Hong Kong, Uruguay and South Africa. The mill ceased production in 1961.

[3] William and Dorothy Wordsworth lived here at Old Windebrowe in 1794, shortly after William's sojourn to France. William Calvert owned the 16th-century farmhouse, and Wordsworth was nursing his brother, Raisley, through a terminal illness. When Raisley died, he bequeathed William enough money to concentrate on a career as a poet. The house is now owned by the Calvert Trust, which provides riding and outdoor activities for the disabled. Two rooms are open to the public. See Appendix 2 for the address and details.

11

RIVER DERWENT & TONGUE GILL

This river walk is one of my favourites. Despite being in the heart of the most rugged of the Lakeland dales, the walk is a gentle stroll through woods alongside a wonderfully clear and quick moving river. It is followed by an ascent along one of the ancient packhorse routes and then a swift descent through the fields with magnificent views across the valley to Rosthwaite and the mountains beyond.

Distance and terrain: 5.3km (3.25 miles). Generally easy walking. The steepest part is the descent across fields from Tongue Gill. This can get muddy and slippery in wet weather.

Parking: National Trust pay-and-display car park, along the lane opposite Rosthwaite post office (GR 258148). Or park next door at the Borrowdale Institute. Parking is very restricted in both locations.

L eaving the car park, turn right and follow the narrow lane away from the centre of the village. You pass several pretty stone cottages and come to a fork in the road at Yew Tree Farm. Go right, over the cobbled farmyard (signed 'Footpath to Grange') and along a rough farm track between the fields. If it is the right time of year, look out for the sheep shearing pens on the right.

The track swings right at the river and leads you to a new-looking packhorse bridge. Notice the way the stone work has been constructed. The last tree on the left, before the bridge, is a rather nice pollarded willow.

Once across the bridge, turn right, along the track to a pair of farm gates. Go through the right-hand gate and keep to the river bank. The Derwent is very powerful when in spate, washing stones and small boulders out into the surrounding fields and you can see the embankments where the river bank has been reinforced.

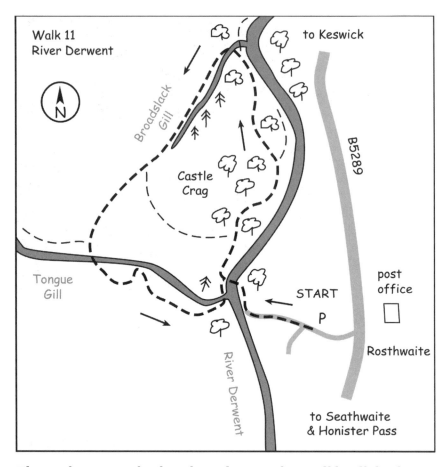

Walk 11
River Derwent

N

Broadslack Gill

to Keswick

B5289

Castle Crag

Tongue Gill

START

P

post office

Rosthwaite

River Derwent

to Seathwaite
& Honister Pass

The track crosses a beck and winds around a small knoll, leading to High Hows Wood. Once through the kissing gate, you are in a lovely old mixed woodland, the trees on your left rising up the lower flanks of Castle Crag [1].

After crossing two small becks, the path appears to split. The right fork takes you for a lovely grassy stroll along the river bank, a delightful way to examine the blue pools and rocks and the mysterious ox-bow bends. This feels like real exploration and is great for kids. Unfortunately, it is also a dead-end – a moss-covered rock outcrop of rock blocks the route. (I'm not recommending you do this but if you have a head for heights it is possible to climb the sloping back of the rock for a tremendous and unusual view of the surround-

The River Derwent at Grange, Borrowdale *(Bill Stainton)*

ing valley, standing above the tree tops. A photographer who was walking with me got very excited when we discovered this view and he promptly lost a lens cap.)

Back to the main path and continue through the woods to the quarry. The path winds past a large cairn, built from the slate rubble that covers the fell side just here [2]. Beyond the slate tip, the path climbs to a T-junction. Go right, downhill between two rocks and through an old stone wall and out of the woods. Turn right again and follow the clear path downhill.

The path leads to a broad track. Continue straight and you rejoin the river. This again is a lovely stretch of the walk. The river is very broad and deep along here and in summer it is a good spot for swimming. It is a pity about the noise from the road on the far bank.

Continue over a stile and the path drops to a wooden footbridge over Broadslack Gill, which feeds into the Derwent at this point. At the signpost turn left (Seatoller, Honister), up a stony path, leaving the River Derwent behind.

You are now following an ancient packhorse route [3] (as used by ancient packhorses, of course). The route climbs the fell, crossing the river now and again. Goat Crag makes an impressive skyline on

49

your right, once you emerge from the woods. Keep straight, ignoring the path left which climbs Castle Crag.

As you cross the beck for the final time and arrive at a group of three sheep pens, there is a superb view of Glaramara ahead of you. Stop and turn round for an even better view, taking in Derwent Water, Skiddaw and the distinctive shape of Castle Head [4], the volcano-shaped hill to the right of the lake.

100m from the sheep pens, there is a marker post and the path splits. Go left, down the narrower path, which takes you to the wooden footbridge over Tongue Gill. As you walk down, the view on the left opens up and you can see across the fields to Rosthwaite and Watendlath fell.

Tongue Gill can be a raging torrent after heavy rainfall and is very impressive. Yet this is a comparatively little-known route, most walkers preferring to come down closer to Castle Crag.

Cross the two footbridges to the gate and stile. 30m beyond the stile, a farm track crosses the path. Go left down the track to the wooden farm gate. Once through the gate, the track leads down a steep field. Again, this can be slippery and muddy after heavy rain. The track meanders somewhat but if in doubt keep Rosthwaite directly ahead of you. You can see the River Derwent below, winding across the pattern of fields.

The track takes you past a stone wall (and a sign pointing right to Scale Close Coppice and Seatoller) and down to a stile in the far right-hand corner of the field beside Tongue Gill. Over the stile and footbridge and you cross two more fields, keeping to the river bank. Eventually you'll come to a final stile as Tongue Gill joins the River Derwent. Over the stile and there are two footbridges in front of you. Go right if you want to explore the opposite bank to the outward part of the trip (but be warned: you have to ford the river to get back to Rosthwaite). Alternatively, cross the left footbridge and the path takes you to New Bridge again. Turn right over the bridge and follow the track back to the starting point.

NOTES

[1] Unlikely though it seems, Borrowdale is named after Castle Crag. The 290m (950ft) summit was a hill fort over 2000 years ago. It is in an ideal position, strategically placed where the valley narrows and the mountains rise precipitously on either side known to the early,

18th-century tourists as the Jaws of Borrowdale. Roman and Samarian pottery has been found on the site but the remains of the hill fort have long since been destroyed by quarrying. Castle Crag was given to the National Trust in 1920 by Sir William Hamer and there is a memorial plaque to him on a seat, visible as you climb the crag. And the name? Borrowdale comes from the old Norse word, borgarárdalr – the valley of the fort.

[2] Stone was quarried in this area until the 1930s. It was also the home of an eccentric mountaineer named Millican Dalton, who lived in a nearby cave and liked to be known as the Professor of Adventure. He was born in Alston in 1867 and worked as a shipping clerk in London, before effectively dropping out to return to the love of his life, the mountains. He was a mountain guide in Scotland, the Lakes and Switzerland and spent the summer months living in his cave. He was vegetarian and made his own clothes, earning an income by giving lessons in climbing and raft building. A famous photograph of him aboard his home-built raft, Rogue Herries, was a best-selling postcard and can still be seen hanging on the wall in Keswick cafés. Dalton died in 1947 but if you search for it, you can still find his cave. It has an inscription above the entrance: "Don't!! waste words, or jump to conclusions."

[3] Packhorse routes cross the Lake District, connecting the major dales and providing trading routes. Many of these date back to the 1100s when wool had to be transported from the farms owned by Furness Abbey, near Barrow-in-Furness, and Fountains Abbey in Yorkshire. The routes continued to be used into the 19th century until the road networks became established and, later, railways were developed.

[4] Castle Head really is a volcanic plug. It is a superb viewpoint and there is a viewfinder on top, which names the surrounding mountains.

12

EASEDALE TARN

Although Easedale Tarn is isolated in the fells above Grasmere, it is easy to reach from the village. It is a popular walk for beginner fell-walkers, with a real feel of being in the mountains. This route begins in Far Easedale, allowing you to enjoy the peace and quiet before climbing to Easedale Tarn and encountering the crowds who have ascended from Grasmere.

Distance and terrain: 7.5km (4.5 miles), including the 1.5km circuit of the tarn). Straightforward walking for the most part, a steep climb to Easedale Tarn and some rough ground during the descent.

Parking: There is a small pay-and-display car park at the top of Easedale Road (the lane beside the Heaton Cooper Gallery). Alternatively, use the National Park car park in the village, just north of the shops on the B5287.

Walk along Easedale Road, away from the village centre. Opposite the car park, there is a stile and a short section of permissive footpath, which takes you off the road. You rejoin the road at Goody Bridge and just past the farm, the road swings right. The footbridge in the trees on your right is going to be on the return route, so don't be tempted by the sign to Easedale Tarn. Continue along the road, past Lancrigg Hotel, and the road takes you across a field, with the sharp pinnacle of Helm Crag [1] directly ahead of you.

Once past a small cluster of houses (including the engagingly named Little Parrock), you come to a fork. Go right (signed 'Far Easedale and Helm Crag'), onto a rough track which leads up to a metal farm gate. Go through the farm gate (ignoring the sign on your right, which lures you off to the Wordsworth memorial and the

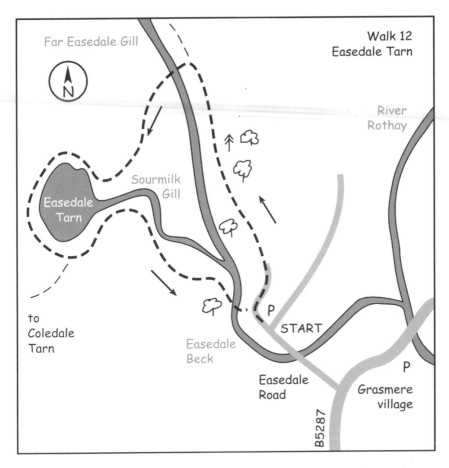

Far Easedale Gill

Walk 12
Easedale Tarn

N

River
Rothay

Sourmilk
Gill

Easedale
Tarn

to
Coledale
Tarn

Easedale
Beck

START

P

P

Easedale
Road

Grasmere
village

B5287

hikers' tea barn) and then bear left to another fork in the path. Go left, signed 'Far Easedale and Borrowdale' [2].

The path takes you between some fine examples of dry stone walls and across a number of fields. It is an easy route to follow. One intriguing point – who thought to plant a monkey-puzzle tree out here in the middle of nowhere? (It is by the field entrance, just before you reach two stone barns on your right.)

This path feels very isolated. When you reach the stone barns, you can glance across the valley to see the swarm of dots heading up the more direct route to Easedale tarn.

A few minutes after the barns, you reach Far Easedale Gill, which is a pleasant, bubbling companion as you follow it upstream. (If your companion is bubbling but not a stream, you should seek medical assistance at the earliest opportunity.)

The path brings you to a long wooden, footbridge. Cross over and you can see the footpath to Borrowdale winding across the fell ahead of you, disappearing into the head of the valley. 40m from the bridge, the path forks. Go left and climb steeply past a split boulder and a footpath marker.

The path climbs to the top of the field on your left, then, at another pair of marker posts, it veers off to the right. Keep climbing and after ten minutes or so you come to Sourmilk Gill [3] and another view of the main path to the tarn. Keeping to your side of the gill, follow the path around the boggy bits. Dogs are very useful here as they tend to rush ahead and you can tell by the various splashing noises which routes to avoid.

This boggy section gets horribly wet in winter and there are occasional lines of stepping stones. Not enough, however, so don't hesitate to abandon the path and climb to firmer ground when you need to. The path is running roughly parallel to the river, although it is out of view most of the time, concealed by the bracken. The path finally approaches the gill and then suddenly you arrive at Easedale Tarn [4].

The tarn is very pretty, with impressive crags on three sides: from the left, these are Blea Crag, Slapestone Edge, Tarn Crag and Greathead Crag. There is usually a seagull perched on the rock in the centre of the tarn. You could cross the beck and head straight downhill but if it is relatively dry underfoot, it is worth circling the tarn. Heading anticlockwise around the tarn, the perspective changes dramatically. As you reach the far side, the path climbs to avoid boggy sections and you should work your way up to a major footpath which continues out of Easedale and on to Stickle Tarn and the Langdales. Once you hit the path, turn left and follow the route back to Sourmilk Gill. The entire circuit takes about half an hour.

As you reach the Gill, the path forks. Go right or you could end up circling the tarn forever. After walking downhill for 20m you have a tremendous view of Helm Crag and Grasmere, with Fairfield on the far side of the valley.

The route downhill is fairly straightforward, though rough underfoot in places. After fifteen minutes or so you come to the first of the cascades in Sourmilk Gill. The rock pools just below are great for a paddle on a hot summer day.

Upper Easedale *(Bill Stainton)*

The path drops down to a stone wall, through a kissing gate and joins a farm track across the fields. Keep to the track, through an ornate metal farm gate and across another field. At the far side, over a concrete bridge, there are two farm gates. Go through the left gate and back alongside Easedale Beck. The path leads into the woods, takes you across a footbridge and you are back at Easedale Road by the Lancrigg Hotel. Go right and seek out one of the tea shops in the village.

NOTES

[1]   Helm Crag has a couple of alternative names derived from the silhouettes formed by the craggy summit. The Lion and the Lamb can be seen from Dunmail Raise, or, from Easedale Tarn, it becomes The Old Lady at the Organ. Heap of Old Rocks doesn't seem to have caught the local imagination.

[2]   There are a number of very long established trading routes which link the valleys, and once you get on the tops it is easy to lose your way and come down in the wrong place. Friends of mine at a local guest house occasionally rescue guests who set off walking to Langdale,

come down in Borrowdale and are faced with an expensive taxi ride back to Grasmere.

[3] Sourmilk (or Sour Milk) is a popular name. There are three Sour Milk Gills in the Lake District, and on the subject of nomenclature, 'gill' is derived from an old Norse word for a wooded valley containing a stream. Wordsworth popularised the spelling 'ghyll', which looks more romantic but is now going out of fashion.

[4] Easedale was well known to William and Dorothy Wordsworth when they lived at Dove Cottage, Grasmere. They called it 'the black quarter' because all the bad weather seemed to come from this direction. A local inn keeper built a refreshment hut by Easedale Tarn and sold teas, carried up in an urn. He even hired out a rowing boat. The hut was demolished in the 1960s and its remains now form the cairn on the far side of the river. A painting of the tarn and hut hangs in Dove Cottage.

13

LEVERS WATER & CHURCH BECK

Levers Water stands in a natural cove, on the side of the Old Man of Coniston. Once a natural tarn, it has been dammed and enlarged to provide power for the mining operations in Coppermines Valley. This route ascends alongside the Levers Waterfall, circuits the tarn and comes down via Boulder Valley and Church Beck. Although hard going in places, you are rewarded with wonderful views of Coniston and a chance to explore a landscape rich in industrial heritage.

Distance and terrain: 7.5km (4.75 miles). A long climb to Levers Water, with some sections of rough track. The circuit of Levers Water may be wet and boggy in places. An easy descent.

Parking: The National Park car park in the centre of the Coniston village, on the B5285 (follow the signs for the tourist information centre).

The walk begins at the centre of the village. Head down Yewdale Road and turn left opposite the post office, up a cul-de-sac between the Black Bull Hotel and the Co-op store. The road runs alongside Church Beck and you are quickly out of the village and surrounded by fields, heading towards Wetherlam and Long Crag.

The road narrows to a single, rough track and is signed 'Coppermines Youth Hostel'. Note the warning sign for quarries and mines. There are a number of deep shafts in Coppermines Valley. Do not be tempted to go caving.

The lane climbs gradually uphill and once over the cattle grid, you start to get a view back to Coniston Water. The white house on the far shore is Brantwood, the home of John Ruskin [1]. Once past the wood on your left, you get another view of the river and a small waterfall. Just above is Miller Bridge, a good viewpoint. Even better, scramble down and see how this old packhorse bridge has been constructed.

Continue up the track, past another waterfall and you can see the white youth hostel ahead. The path forks; keep straight ahead, towards the YHA. Levers Water Beck on your left is very wide and meanders through a valley wrecked by mining [2]. Vegetation is reclaiming the spoil heaps but it is still a desolate view. Another beck comes in from the right and across that you can see a terrace of houses, once miners' cottages and now used by the Yorkshire Mountaineering Club.

The track bears left, to pass in front of the youth hostel and alongside Levers Water Beck. Look out for the old mining carts scattered about the valley floor. There is an information panel just past the youth hostel. Attempts have been made to establish a museum here but so far the plans have always fallen foul of planning regulations.

Just past a stone hut (the old powder store for the mine), you pass another waterfall and in the hills to the left you can see Low Water Beck tumbling down the fell side. Ahead is the Old Man of Coniston and behind you can still see Coniston Water.

Above the waterfall, the path divides, with the left fork heading down to a rusty iron footbridge. Go right, uphill, leaving the beck behind but climbing towards Levers Waterfall. As you climb you get a view over the desolate foreground to Coniston Water and the pine-covered fells beyond.

The track begins to converge with the river again. After a steady climb for a few minutes, you will arrive at a small plateau and a crossroads in the path. Left goes to a wooden footbridge but you should turn right, zigzagging up the hill, past a small cave (beware trolls) and an open mine shaft. The path gets steeper and is rough underfoot. As you approach the waterfall and the wall of the dam, look back for a brilliant view of Coniston Water, beyond that the Yorkshire Dales and, around to the right, Morecambe Bay. The tower on the hill just in front of the bay is the Barrow Monument at Ulverston, a replica of Eddystone Lighthouse,

Climb up to the dam wall and you arrive at Levers Water [3]. Now you have a choice. You could go left, cross the river and begin descending almost immediately. A more interesting option is to make the 1.5km circuit, anticlockwise around the reservoir. Skirting the shore, the perspective continually changes and with it, the atmo-

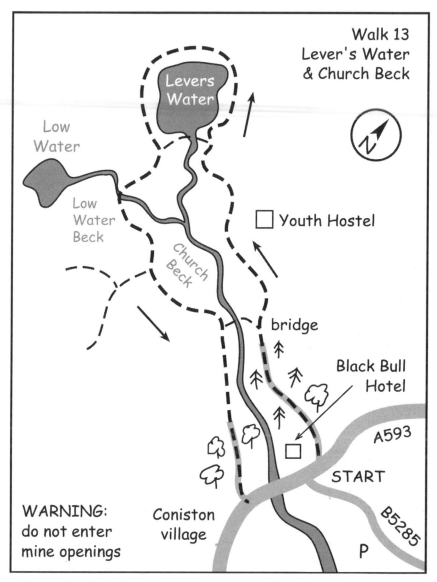

Walk 13
Lever's Water
& Church Beck

Levers
Water

Low
Water

Low
Water
Beck

Church
Beck

☐ Youth Hostel

bridge

Black Bull
Hotel

A593

☐

START

WARNING:
do not enter
mine openings

Coniston
village

B5285

P

N

sphere of this isolated mountain tarn. The crags form a natural amphitheatre and you can hear the voices of walkers as they climb Gill Cove Crag on the far shore.

The path around the tarn is distinct until you reach Swirl Hawse Beck, whereupon it disappears into a bog. Go right down to the shore and you should be able to traverse the rocks and keep your boots dry. Looking back from this point, the solitary rock in the tarn acts like a sight, centred on the view into the valley below. Two thirds of the way round, the shore becomes very squelchy. Climb above the bog and you join a path coming in from the right. Go left and follow the shore towards the dam.

The path is distinct as you enter a boulder field (this whole area is known as Boulder Valley) and approach a spoil tip on the right. Continue below the spoil tip and a path comes in from the right, about 40m before the dam wall. Turn right, back up this path to climb the spoil tip and past the mine opening on the left. This is a mine shaft which has collapsed and left a gaping hole in the hillside. There is a danger sign and the mine entrance is fenced off. Continue up the hill, past a second fence and then bear left up the hill. Don't continue straight or you will end up on the scree. Climb to the saddle between a grassy knoll on your left and the scree on your right, passing a large, flat-topped boulder. Looking back you get a final view of Levers Water.

Once over the saddle, you drop down into the grassy valley, with a superb view of Coniston Water as you descend. Watch out for *Gondola*, the National Trust steam launch.

The grassy slope is littered with boulders and the path zigzags between them, heading towards Low Water Beck below. The view to the left opens up and you can see Coppermines Valley and the youth hostel once more. As you drop down to the beck, there is a large, angular boulder on the left, which looks like something imported from Easter Island. This is good for a practice scramble.

Once across the beck, there is the remains of an old pipeline on the right and another huge boulder, frequently covered in rock climbers.

The path continues across the flanks of the Old Man, crossing another beck and then onto scree. You pass a picturesque mine entrance on the right, with water dripping down the moss-covered rock. It is safe to peer in but do not enter. The path continues below a crag and then reaches a T-junction with a much larger track. Turn left and go downhill. After 20m, the track bears right around the hill and forks. Go straight on, downhill towards the youth hostel, to a gate in a stone wall. Go through the gate, across the field to a gap in another stone wall. Here the path bears left, away from the wall, and continues downhill through the bracken.

The path drops to a wire fence. Follow it down the hill, alongside Levers Water Beck again, through another gate and down to Millers Bridge. You can cross and retrace your steps to the car. Alternatively, continue past the bridge without crossing, and go through a kissing gate. The beck is now on the other side of a stone wall and you drop down along the bottom of a field to a slate workshop. Once past the workshop, the path becomes a track and bears left, keeping to the river. You cross another beck coming in from the right and then pass a lovely wooded spot by the river, complete with a bench. This is a handy spot to sit and get your breath after the long slog down from Boulder Valley [4].

Continue down the track to arrive at Dixon Ground Farm. Go through the gate onto the tarmac road and turn right. At the T-junction, next to the Sun Inn, turn left and follow the road down into the village, emerging beside the road bridge in the centre of Coniston.

NOTES

[1] Brantwood was the home of art-critic, philosopher and social reformer, John Ruskin. He lived here from 1872 to 1900, having bought the property sight unseen for £1500. He transformed a run-down property into a beautiful home and lived here thirty years, until his death. The house is now open to the public and in recent years, with the help of European Union grants, the grounds have been restored to Ruskin's original layout. A fascinating place, it must occupy one of the most beautiful sites in Britain.

[2] Copper has been mined from Coniston Old Man since Roman times. In the 1600s, the German engineers of the Company of Mines Royal dug the area and the copper ore was sent for smelting to the newly built smelting works at Keswick. The mines were at their peak in the 1850s, when 3,000 tons of copper pyrite a year was dug out of the mountain, shafts descending over 300m (1000ft). It was the most important copper mine in Europe, employing over 900 men. Mining declined when pumping water out of the deep shafts became uneconomic. The mines closed in 1915. Coppermines Youth Hostel was once the home and office of the mines manager.

[3] Levers Water is about 38m (125ft) deep and surrounded on three sides by Great Crag, Little Crag and Erin Crag. It is a natural tarn but was dammed and the level raised in order to provide power for the copper mines.

[4] Look carefully and you should be able to see miniature railway signals in the woods on the far side of the beck. This is a private estate owned by a train enthusiast who has built his own miniature line through the woods.

14

RIVER LOWTHER

Some of the nicest countryside in Cumbria lies just outside the boundary of the national park. Less rugged and dramatic than the central Lakes, the area to the east of the park has superb river walks and a variety of delightful villages. This route explores the area around the village of Askham, the beautiful River Lowther and offers a glimpse of what appears to be the gothic ruins of a castle.

Distance and terrain: 8.5km (4.75 miles). An easy, Sunday afternoon kind of stroll.

Parking: There is no car park in Askham but space can usually be found along the main street.

Walking down the centre of Askham village, towards the river, look out for the lane on the left, opposite the Punchbowl Inn. It is by the boundary wall to Askham Hall, just below the village green. Turn along this lane, through the studded wooden gates (signed 'Public Bridleway') and along the track between two stone walls. You'll catch sight of Askham Hall [1] on your right.

The track goes past a barn and workshop to a farm gate. Go through the gate and along the track between the fields. After 200m, look out for the footpath sign on your right. Cross the stile and go diagonally across the field, to the far corner. A ladder stile takes you over the stone wall and into Heining Wood [2].

The path narrows beside a short section of wooden rail (the ground slopes away steeply to your right) and, after another 200m, you begin to head downhill. When the path forks at the next rail, go right and keep a look out for grouse scuttling through the undergrowth.

Drop down now to walk alongside the River Lowther. This is a very pleasant stretch of woodland and when you reach the metal

Kendal Roughs having a dip in the River Lowther *(Bill Stainton)*

gate, it is tempting to carry straight on and continue walking along the tree-lined river bank [3]. However, go through the metal gate and you are on a tarmac lane, running through the woods. Nip straight across for a short diversion and from the splendid vantage point of the river bank you can examine the stone bridge over the River Lowther. The original bridge is no longer able to carry vehicles, so a lower, metal bridge has been built alongside.

Once you are satisfied that the stone bridge is in no danger of imminent collapse, go back up to the tarmac lane and cross the stone bridge via the stiles at either end. (These stiles are amongst the widest I've encountered, obviously designed for the efficient throughput of hordes of ramblers.)

Continue up the tarmac road and you begin to cross the well-tended park of Lowther Estate. After 50m, a strange sight begins to materialise over the distant trees. A row of soaring turrets, a crenellated wall and Lowther Castle [4] rises into view, like a gothic vision from a Disney cartoon.

As you walk up the lane, notice how the oak trees form an avenue either side. When you reach the T-junction at the top of the park, the avenue continues to march ahead, straight across the park towards

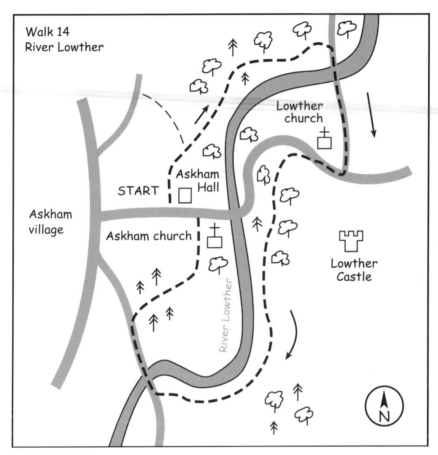

Walk 14
River Lowther

Lowther
church

Askham
START | Hall

Askham
village

Askham church

Lowther
Castle

River Lowther

N

the castle. Turn right at the junction and walk downhill towards the church [5].

Once over the cattle grid by the church, turn immediately left and cross the stile into the field (signed 'Public Footpath'). Bear right, diagonally across the field towards another stile in the fence at the edge of the woods. Once into the woods, the path bears round to the left and continues in nice level fashion, the ground rolling away to your right to the River Lowther. The river itself is out of view but you may be able to spot Askham church again through the trees.

The path is not tremendously well-defined, but to begin with you are running roughly parallel with the fence. It is a very pleasant mixed woodland, with one or two less common species such as sycamore and maple. Look out for red squirrels.

After passing an old stretch of fence, the path begins a gentle descent. Notice the ornate iron bench which curves around the base of an oak on your right. Just past the bench, the path comes to a T-junction. Go left and the path brings you to the old stone wall surrounding the castle gardens.

At the wall, you join a track and head right. 50m further on, the track forks and you should go right, descending through a very pretty wood with tantalising glimpses of the river between the trees. Once you leave the woods via a farm gate, you cross more carefully tended park land and get a brilliant view of the river below you, very wide and gentle, curving against the backdrop of the pine forest on the opposite shore, with the Lakeland fells visible in the distance.

The track heads along the river bank through splendid park land. The wall around the castle grounds run along a limestone bluff on your left, high at the top of the field. Running your eye along, it is tricky spotting where the wall ends and the limestone begins. You can also just see the roof of a pagoda in the grounds, with what appears to be a tree growing through its shingle roof. As you walk beside the river, notice the watering trough, sunk into the hillside to conceal it from view from the castle. This is real park land and it is great to see it in such good condition. There is a lovely sweep of hillside away to your left.

The track brings you to a fence line. Go through the farm gate and the path splits. Go right, keeping to a permissive footpath rather than the right of way. The track follows the bend in the river and arrives at a narrow country lane. Once in the lane, go right, over Crookwath Bridge, and follow the lane back towards Askham.

After walking for about ten minutes, you pass two public footpath signs on either side of the road. Go right, over a stone wall and into a small mixed plantation. At the next gate, cross the stile and go straight along the track, keeping the woods on your left and the fields on your right. You now get a view back across the river and fields to the earlier path and of the limestone escarpment.

When the plantation ends, keep on the track and when it swings left, go straight ahead, over a stile (look out for the yellow marker arrow) and straight across the field, keeping the stone wall on your left. Follow the wall round to another farm gate. Go through the gate and you are walking along the bottom of a field, with another wood on your right. There is a good view of Askham Hall ahead.

Keep to the wire fence on your right and you drop down to a track which emerges from the wood. Go left and into the graveyard via a small wooden gate. You rejoin the river on your right. Still keeping to the line of the metal fence, the path skirts the graveyard and through another gate, into the churchyard [6] proper. You can go either way through the churchyard. If you go right, you get a view of the river and when you emerge on the main road through the village, divert right for the view of Lowther River from Askham Bridge. After that, it's back up the hill to the centre of the village. Careful timing will ensure that the Punchbowl Inn is open.

NOTES

[1] Askham Hall is, unfortunately, not accessible to the public, but you do catch glimpses of this fine house from several points on the walk. Built in the 14th century as a pele tower, it was converted into an Elizabethan mansion in 1574 by Thomas Sandford. It remained in the Sandford family until 1828, when it became the rectory. It is now the home of the Earl of Lonsdale, one of England's greatest landowners. The name of the village, incidentally, means 'the place with the ash trees'.

[2] Like much of the woodland around here, this was planted in the late 1950s and is part of the Lowther estate. 20m into the wood, you come to a junction by a way-marking post. Go left and the path takes you through the trees, just within the edge of the wood. You can hear the River Lowther somewhere through the trees to your right and you may catch a fleeting glimpse of Askham church.

[3] In fact, there is a right of way which allows you to continue along the river from this point. It runs through the woods for a further 2 miles (3.25km) to emerge near Penrith, at the wonderfully named 'King Arthur's Round Table' (an early Bronze Age henge, although Sir Lancelot is rumoured to have killed a giant here). However, to make this a round trip involves a mile of road walking along the A6 – breathing in a variety of fumes from heavy lorries – until you regain a footpath at the village of Clifton. The name Lowther is probably Old Norse (usually a safe bet in Cumbria) and comes from 'lauthra-a' which means 'the foaming river'.

[4] Lowther Castle is a fake. It was built as a magnificent mansion

between 1806 and 1811, commissioned by Sir John Lowther, the fifth Earl of Lonsdale. The architect was Robert Smirke, who went on to design the British Museum. The Lowther Estate has been in the ownership of the Lowther family for more than 700 years, and there was a hall built here in the 13th century. The family lived in Lowther Castle until 1936, when death duties forced them to move out to the more modest accommodation of Askham Hall. The bulk of the building was pulled down, leaving only the impressive facade. A great pity the National Trust didn't get there first.

[5] A church stood on this site in the 12th century but the present St Michael's is mostly Victorian. It is the family burial place of the Lowther family and, in 1857, they added the mausoleum in the churchyard. The head of the Lowther family holds the hereditary title of Earl of Lonsdale. The fifth Earl, Sir John Lowther, sponsored the Lonsdale Belt in boxing. He was known as the Yellow Earl, not for any lack of bravery but because his favourite colour was yellow. He made all his servants wear the colour and passed it onto the Automobile Association, when he became their first president.

[6] There was a church on this site, dedicated to St Columba, in the 13th century. The present church is dedicated to St Peter and was rebuilt by Robert Smirke in 1832. Inside are memorials to the Sandford family. Robert Southey's son, Charles, was vicar here until his death in 1888.

15

TAYLORGILL FORCE & SPRINKLING TARN

This is an excellent, if strenuous, mountain walk from the heart of Borrowdale, the most rugged and dramatic of the Lakeland dales. A sharp climb takes you up to Taylorgill Force, for my money the most spectacular waterfall in Cumbria. From there it is an easy climb to Styhead and Sprinkling tarns, in the midst of the mountains. Finally, you make a straightforward descent via Grains Gill with spectacular views of Borrowdale, Derwent Water and the northern fells.

Distance and terrain: 9km (5.2 miles) – add an extra 1.4km (1 mile) if starting from Seathwaite Bridge. This is the most strenuous walk in the book, involving a steep climb to Taylorgill Force along a path which is rough and unstable. Following the route in the direction described, leaves the easier gradient for the descent, with more freedom to take in the view. Use proper walking boots with ankle support and good grip. A good head for heights is useful.

Parking: Limited parking available on the roadside on the approach to Seathwaite Farm.

There are two alternatives for the start of the walk.

STARTING POINT 1

If you are close to the farm, or have arrived by bus, follow the lane to Seathwaite Farm and go straight into the farm yard. Note that the farmhouse does teas if you are back in time. A few metres into the farmyard, there is an archway in the barn on your right. Go through and follow the track between the fields to a footbridge. Cross and the footpath splits three ways. Go left, through the wooden gate, and proceed from 'WALK CONTINUES HERE', below.

STARTING POINT 2

If you have arrived late and have been forced to park further from the farm, you can avoid the road altogether. Walk back over Seathwaite road bridge and then turn immediately left, through a small wooden gate (signed 'Public Footpath'). Cross the stile next to the farm gate and then follow the path along the river bank. The path heads upstream, winds through bracken and past a conifer plantation. As you walk the path, notice the heavily reinforced riverbank on the far side; this area has the highest measured rainfall in the Lake District. You eventually arrive at a wooden farm gate. Go through the gate and along the bank to a wooden footbridge over Sourmilk Gill. The path splits three ways here. Left crosses the footbridge to Seathwaite Farm [1]. Go straight, through the small gate in the stone wall.

WALK CONTINUES HERE

The path sticks to the bank of the river. In summer the river is reduced to a trickle but come here after a winter thaw and it is a major force of nature. Look up the fell to the right and you may spot climbers practising on a distinctive outcrop of rock.

The path gets rougher and goes past a conifer plantation. Look out for butterwort along here, a fleshy green carnivorous plant. The path climbs gradually to leave the conifers behind, winding up a fell side field. You cross another wall via a ladder stile and then begin to climb more steeply. You have left the river below now but the path is still distinct, although boggy in places. Through another old wall and turn back for a view of Blencathra and the motorway coming down from Watendlath.

The path crosses an outcrop of rock and as you approach the gully you begin to hear the rush of water. Within a dozen metres the view of Taylorgill Force is astonishing. The path now gets very rough and winds steeply below a crag to what must be the Lake Districts shortest stone wall. It juts out from the crag on your right, runs a few metres to the drop to the gully and stops. Go through the gate and you find yourself climbing along a precipitous path over-

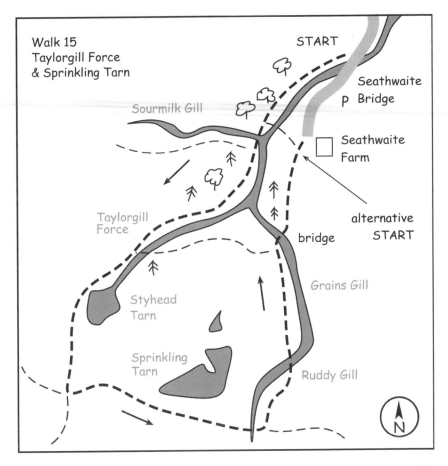

Walk 15
Taylorgill Force
& Sprinkling Tarn

START

Seathwaite
p Bridge

Sourmilk Gill

Seathwaite
Farm

Taylorgill
Force

alternative
START

bridge

Grains Gill

Styhead
Tarn

Sprinkling
Tarn

Ruddy Gill

N

looking the gully, a sheer drop to your left. Concentrate on the magnificent view of the waterfall ahead and it may keep your mind off the fact that a great deal of this path is permanently on the move.

The path drops to a stone wall, then climbs again. You're now following a wall and walking uphill, climbing level with the waterfall. This is a good opportunity to look back at the path you've just followed and the view down into the ravine. Where the stone wall becomes a wire fence, there is a stile and you can cross to a shady picnic spot in the trees, right at the head of Taylorgill Force [2].

Back on the path, continue climbing past the trees and into the head of an open, V-shaped valley. There is a dramatic view on the left of Aaron Crag; with Glaramara further round. The severe cleft in

Hind Side is cut by Red Beck. You may see walkers on the far side of the beck, following the bridleway, a pack-horse route between Borrowdale and Wasdale.

As you approach the top of the valley, the stream forms cascades and one or two attractive pools. The path forks, with the left route crossing the river to descend the bridleway to Stockley Bridge and Seathwaite.

Continue straight on, ignoring the wooden footbridge, and past a large cairn in the middle of an old stream bed, over a couple more becks and eventually to Styhead Tarn.

Taylorgill Force near Seathwaite, Borrowdale *(Bill Stainton)*

This is a very pretty little tarn, overlooked by the massive grey bulk of Great End. On the right is Lingmell, then Scafell Pike, Broad End and back to Great End. A popular camping spot, it is an ideal spot to launch yourself up a range of major Lakeland mountains.

Continue past Styhead Tarn, along a made path and up to the crest of the ridge [3]. You immediately encounter a large wooden box, the mountain rescue post at Sty Head. To save you the bother of looking, this contains first aid gear and a metal sled, used to convey injured walkers and climbers rapidly down the fell.

This is a major crossroads of routes. From here you could climb Scafell Pike, England's highest mountain, drop to Wasdale and Wast

Water, the deepest of the sixteen lakes. Or, you could go left and head to Sprinkling Tarn. Keep your eyes peeled and 200m from the rescue box, if conditions are good you can catch a glimpse of the Irish Sea.

After ten minutes, you have climbed from Sty Head to walk alongside a small beck. It splashes down a narrow gully, lined with parsley fern. The path crosses the beck, there is another short climb and then you suddenly find yourself at Sprinkling Tarn [4]. This is a wild, isolated tarn, surrounded by mountain peaks. To the south are Great End and the Scafell range, to the west Lingmell and Great Gable.

Continue past the tarn, over the ridge and you drop to the head of Ruddy Gill (so named because of the high iron content of the soil). The path which goes over the gill and straight ahead would take you to Angle Tarn and down into Langdale valley. This would be a bit inconvenient if you've parked at Seathwaite. Instead, cross the gill which is an eroded gully just here and turn left, down along the narrow ravine on your left. A superb view opens up; as you descend you can see Blencathra in the distance, then a tremendous view of Skiddaw and Derwent Water, with Castle Crag in the middle distance.

The ravine is a dark cleft in the rocks, covered in a variety of mosses, lichens and ferns, despite the efforts of ill-educated gill scramblers.

It is a long walk down but it is made easier by the well-constructed path and the wonderful view. You cross Ruddy Gill via a wooden footbridge and then Grains Gill comes in from the right. Ignore the next footbridge and continue down to a wooden gate in a stone wall. Once through, follow the wall downhill until you reach a gate and stone bridge. Go right, through the gate and over Stockley Bridge [5].

As you continue downhill, you catch a glimpse of Taylorgill Force again. The path drops to a stile over a wire fence and continues downstream. Notice the long wall running along the fell on the far side; this stops adventurous local sheep escaping to the exotic climes of Ennerdale.

The path drops to the right of a funny, narrow conifer plantation and you lose sight of the river again. Continue straight, between the field boundaries and through two more farm gates and finally into the farm yard at Seathwaite. The right of way goes left, past the farm house and sheep pens. (If you've arrived down here late, note that there is a telephone box on the right.) You can either go left, through the archway and back along the river to Seathwaite Bridge, or straight through the farmyard to the road.

NOTES

[1] Seathwaite has the dubious distinction of being the wettest inhabited place in Britain, with an annual rainfall of over 3m (125 inches). Measurements have been taken here since Victorian times.

[2] Probably the Lake District's finest waterfall, Taylorgill Force plummets 42m (137ft) down a cleft in the rocks to provide a spectacle known locally as the White Maid of Borrowdale. The force marks the edge of a hanging valley created during the last Ice Age.

[3] Sty Head Pass is a junction for several major mountain routes. There was once a proposal to take a road through here, linking Borrowdale with the west coast of Cumbria. The idea was last rejected by Cumberland County Council in 1934.

[4] Sprinkling Tarn beats even Seathwaite for rainfall; over 5m (200 inches) a year has been recorded here. The tarn's Old English name was Prentibountern, which meant 'sparkling stream', and for a time it was known as Sparkling Tarn.

[5] A sturdy, traditionally built structure, Stockley Bridge stands on the packhorse route between Borrowdale and Wasdale. This is not the original bridge, which was severely damaged in storms in August 1966, when 130mm (5ins) of rain fell in an hour. Just below the bridge is an excellent pool, popular with bathers after the long descent from Scafell Pike.

THE LAKES

Grasmere from Loughrigg Terrace *(Graham Beech)*

16

CONISTON WATER

The south-west corner of Coniston, around Blawith and Torver, has a character distinct from anywhere else in the Lakes. Bracken covered common, rushing becks lined with juniper and above it all the magnificent presence of Coniston Old Man. It is also wonderfully secluded and although the road sometimes gets busy, a few hundred metres onto the common and you are in a world of your own. This route covers one of the best walks on Torver Common, combining it with a walk along Coniston's wonderful shore line.

Distance and terrain: 6km (3.5 miles). The first part of the walk (along the shore) is relatively easy, the second, up to Torver Tarn, is harder, involving a moderate climb. As the circuit is almost a figure-of-eight, it is possible to treat it as two separate walks, linked by a short stretch of road.

Parking: Park at Torver, Beckstones, opposite the Lakeland Land Rover garage (GR 286933), 1km (0.6 miles) south of Torver on the A5084 to Lowick. There is additional parking at the half way point of the walk, around 500m south of Beckstones at GR 287927.

A s you face the car park, back towards the Land Rover garage, the path leaves via the top left corner. A track leads up to a farm gate and kissing gate and once through you are on Torver Common and National Park Authority access land. There is a beck immediately in front of you; don't cross but go left and follow the less distinct track by the stone wall. This brings you to the first of the three tarns on this walk, Kelly Hall Tarn, a small, reedy affair in a shallow bowl in the moor.

Continue left, past the corner of the wall and you come to a good view of Coniston Old Man, the craggy ridge of Dow Crag running

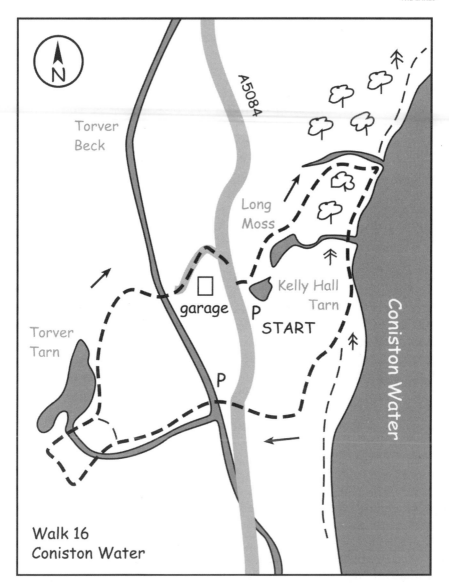

Walk 16
Coniston Water

into it from the left. The path works around a rocky knoll, keeping to a second stone wall and fence on your left. When you reach the corner of the wall, the path splits two ways. The Ordnance Survey would have you go left, but this route can be boggy and difficult to follow. Besides, that way you would miss one of the best views in the area. So go straight on, following the distinct, narrow path along the edge of the hill on your right. You are walking towards what at first appears to be a pathetic, boggy pond but as you approach, your high viewpoint reveals it to be a long, narrow tarn known as Long Moss. Keep going and suddenly the view opens out by the time you reach the end of the hill, level with the foot of Long Moss, you have a superb panorama which takes in Coniston Water, the Old Man and, beyond, Fairfield and the central Lakeland fells. The view to the left is particularly fine as the road is concealed in the valley and there is little sign of human habitation, just rolling, bracken-covered moor leading your eye to the distinctive peak of the Old Man. Looking along the moor, there is a sharp pinnacle above the bracken, over-looking the lake. The green path to the left of it is going to be our route.

Follow the path down the hill, past the end of Long Moss and across the moor, roughly parallel to Coniston Water [1]. The route is a little indistinct at times. It goes down through a little valley and then up to the pinnacle, passing a holly tree on your left. Walk past the famous pinnacle (an outcrop of rock well worth climbing for another fabulous view) and head straight towards the distant moun-tains. The path begins to go downhill and you can see the head of Coniston Water, Brantwood in the distance, on the far shore, and the Coniston Boating Centre just visible in the north west corner of the lake.

After 40m or so, another path comes in from the left. Go right, parallel to a stone wall and a powerful beck and you walk through a veritable forest of juniper. Keep to the right-hand bank of the stream and it leads you down to a wire fence and a farm gate. Once through, you are in a pleasant, coppiced woodland, planted on the steeply sloping side of Torver Common. The path peels off from the beck and follows a stone wall which stands between you and a pretty larch wood.

The path drops to the lake shore. Go right and you follow a delightful lake shore path. Although you have your back to the fells along this path, there are good views to the foot of the lake. Look out for sailing dinghies and the magnificent National Trust *Gondola* [2].

The path passes a number of small bays and pebble beaches. There is no evidence of a road on the far shore but you may hear the occasional car and sometimes, on a still day, the voices of picnick-

The Steam Yacht Gondola *(Graham Beech)*

ers. This is an idyllic little path and is rapidly becoming one of my favourite lake shore footpaths. The route is level, easy to follow and there is nothing to distract you from admiring the views over the water.

You leave the wood behind and the path continues along the shore, open common above you to the right. This means the views get even better, though it is only for a short while as you plunge into a copse of trees. After half an hour of steady walking, you pass a small bench seat: brilliant for picnics and a good vantage point for *Gondola* spotting. You are directly opposite the pier at Park-a-moor. Look a little to the right and you can make out Peel Island [3].

100m beyond the bench, the path leaves the shore and climbs the hill, just as you reach a stone wall. Notice the stone boat house on the far side. The path levels out and runs alongside the wall for a short distance, passing a silver birch which clings to the top of a rock outcrop, right by the path how on earth does it stay on? 100m past the silver birch, the path becomes over excited and fans out in all directions. Unless you double back on yourself, it doesn't really matter which route you take. The easiest is to stay with the wall a little longer, then the path bends right, past a small pond, and climbs alongside a wire fence to a farm gate and kissing gate.

Go through the gate and follow the path right, across the common. You are nearing the road again, so gather in any children and domestic wildlife. The path begins to drop and you can look across the valley to the river and a footpath on the far side of the road. You are going to be climbing that steep hill in front of you, in a few minutes (unless you opt for the short option, below).

The path drops to the road, beside a small car parking space. Now for the short option: If you are running out of time or members of the party are beginning to flag, you can curtail the walk at this point by turning right an following the road 500m back to the Land Rover garage. No one need ever know and you can always come back and do the second half of the walk another day.

For those of you wanting to do the complete walk, go straight across the road to a kissing gate (signed 'Public Footpath') and another National Park Authority sign for Torver Common. The path drops down a gorse-covered field and after 60m you arrive at Torver Beck. This is a fast flowing river and it is sometimes possible to cross via stepping stones. However, the NPA have installed an excellent footbridge just 20m upstream. As you cross the beck to the alder-lined far bank, look out for dippers.

Once over the stile at the end of the footbridge, the path splits three ways. Go straight, up the open fell side, following Mere Beck upstream. This beck is lined with juniper in fact this must have once been a juniper wood, now long since cleared by charcoal burners. Note the electricity poles; this is one of the few areas of the Lake District where the ground is so rocky it has been impossible to run the cables underground. The bright yellow Danger of Death stickers on each pole don't do a great deal to enhance the landscape.

You follow the line of the poles uphill, passing a small land slip on the left. Look out for the wild rose bush, just as you cross a small beck. Just past a small peat bog, the path moves away from the river and forks. Right is a narrow, eroded path. Go left and a wide, 20m path brings you to another beck and a little cascade.

Over the beck and up the hill and, after another 70m, the path swings right and joins the narrow eroded path you've just spurned. Go left, up a slight rise and you have a surprise view of the tarn, in the foreground, with the magnificent spectacle of Coniston Old Man and Wetherlam in the distance.

The left path takes you below the electric cables again and down to the shore of Torver Tarn [4], next to the old reservoir wall. The path swings up onto the hill on the right, continuing parallel to the tarn. Ahead you can see the houses of Torver village and another cracking view of the Old Man, with Holme Fell and Loughrigg in the distance.

The path takes you down the hill, past the end of the tarn and towards two converging stone walls. The view is somewhat spoilt by the messy Land Rover garage. I wish they would plant a few trees to screen it. The path brings you to a farm gate where the walls almost meet. Down the narrow track and it takes you alongside the fields, past a bank barn and onto a narrow lane beside Mill Bridge.

The neat white house opposite is built on the site of an old mill (look for the mill stone beside the gate). The route goes across the bridge, but first it is worth going up the bridle path to the left of the house, through the gate and into the wood. Look down through the woods and you can see the feeder stream and sluice gate for the waterwheel. Go back, and cross the bridge. There is a pleasant, tranquil mill pond on your right as you cross, surrounded by trees.

Once over the bridge, go left and as you pass through the farm gate, look back into the trees and you can see the remains of the mill building and overshot waterwheel.

Continue up the track to the main road. Go right, past Emlin Hall and the road brings you back to the car park and starting point.

NOTES

[1] Coniston Water is one of four lakes designated a public highway. The ore from Coppermines Valley used to be transported down the lake and loaded aboard ships at Greenodd, when that village was a thriving port (before the estuary silted up). Its status as a highway has never been rescinded, which means that powered craft are permitted to use it though, fortunately (in my opinion) speed restrictions now deter power boats from blasting along its length. The lake was originally known as Thorstein's Water, after one of Lakeland's many Norse settlers. It is 8km (5 miles) long, 0.8km (0.5 miles) wide and 55m (175ft) at its deepest point.

Coniston Water was the scene of Donald Campbell's ill-fated world water speed record attempt in 1967. In his boat, *Bluebird*, he had already set a record of 202.32mph on Ullswater in 1955 and raised it to over 280mph on Coniston Water in 1966. During his final attempt, on 4 January 1967, the official timekeepers recorded a speed of 318mph before *Bluebird*, only 43m (140ft) from

The memorial to Donald Campbell on the shore of Coniston Water *(Graham Beech)*

the final marker, soared into the air, somersaulted and vanished into the water. The wreckage of *Bluebird* was recovered in March 2001, followed by the recovery of the remains of Donald Campbell two months later. There is a slate memorial in Coniston village and a further one is located near the Bluebird Café, this being a temporary headstone originally at the grave of Donald Campbell.

[2] The *Gondola* is unequivocally the nicest form of powered transport in the Lake District. (I might be tempted to extend that to the whole country.) Launched in 1860 as a passenger craft and run by the Furness Railway Company, this 25.8m (84ft) long craft was built in Liverpool at a cost of £1000 and transported to Coniston Water in sections. Gondola continued as a passenger boat until 1936, after which it was used as a house boat for a while before being wrecked by a storm in the 1960s. The National Trust rescued the craft from the scrap heap, only to sink it again to preserve the iron hull until funds were available to restore it. After a magnificent research and restoration job, the refitted Gondola was launched in 1980.

[3] The area around Torver and the southern end of Coniston Water should be familiar to all Arthur Ransome fans. His famous children's book, 'Swallows and Amazons' was based around here, although

Ransome changed most of the names. The basic geography stayed the same and in her excellent book, 'Arthur Ransome and Captain Flint's Trunk', Christina Hardyment tracked down most of the original locations. Peel Island is the site of the Secret Harbour and Wild Cat Island, the River Crake is the Amazon, Allan Tarn is Octopus Lagoon and the Old Man is Kanchenjunga. Further afield, Bowness became Rio and Belle Isle was Long Island.

Ransome went to school in Windermere and lived for part of his exceptionally adventurous adult life near Coniston. He died in 1967 and is buried in Rusland churchyard. At the Museum of Lakeland Life and Industry, Kendal, there is a recreation of his study, featuring Ransome's original desk.

[4] Torver Tarn lies in open moorland, the result of extensive deforestation in the 16th century, to provide fuel for the local iron bloomery. Despite the low wall, it is a natural tarn, the damming having been done to increase the water supply to a nearby bobbin mill.

This can be a wild spot, the wind whipping across the moor and humming in the overhead wires. But on a sunny, summer day it is glorious, strolling along beside the water, the dramatic peaks in the distance.

17

BUTTERMERE

This is a classic circuit of the prettiest of the smaller lakes. It is possible to keep to the lake shore for most of the route, with an ever changing perspective of the surrounding mountains. This is an ideal walk for families and anyone wanting a rest from the high fells.

Distance and terrain: 6.4km (4 miles). Mostly level, with a short steep climb above the tunnel section.

Parking: National Park pay-and-display car park, behind the Bridge Hotel. Be warned, this gets full very early in summer. There is an additional lay-by on the Newlands road but please don't park on the grass verges.

From the National Park car park, go past the Bridge Hotel, back to the main road, and turn right towards Syke Farm. Follow the track into the farmyard (signed 'Public Bridleway, Lake Shore Path'), between the houses and out via the stile by the farm gate (signed 'Footpath'). Once past the farm you get a good view of Buttermere, High Stile the fell above the far shore and Sourmilk Gill, the waterfall in the trees. This is a good way to avoid the queues as most walkers tend to take the anticlockwise route round the lake.

The path takes you through a field to another farm gate. Go right, following the sign for the lake shore path and down a path between the field boundaries. At the bottom, go through another gate and down a short flight of stone steps. The path takes you round the edge of the field to a kissing gate and the entrance to Pike Rigg woods. Through another kissing gate and you are on the lake shore [1].

The trees restrict your view of the lake to begin with but this quickly turns into a lovely, easy walk along the wooded lake shore. Shortly after the third kissing gate, look out for the view of Hay Stacks and Warnscale Beck at the far end of the lake. Hay Stacks is

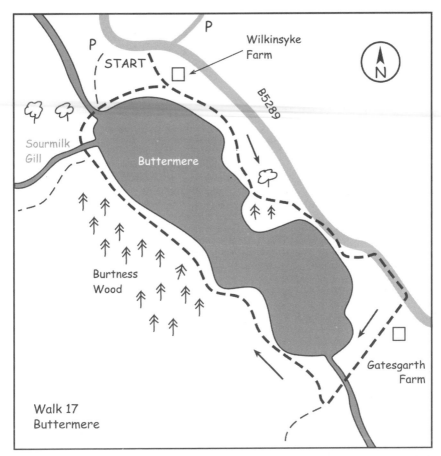

P

P
/START\

Wilkinsyke
Farm

B5289

N

Sourmilk
Gill

Buttermere

Burtness
Wood

Gatesgarth
Farm

Walk 17
Buttermere

an excellent walk and was the favourite of the pioneer fell walker and guide book writer, Alfred Wainwright. After his death in 1991, his ashes were scattered on the mountain. There is a memorial to him in Buttermere church.

The route becomes like a garden path, level and easy to follow. After kissing gate number four, the route goes through park land and past a group of lime trees. This is a good route for tree spotting – look out for sycamore, oak, lime and the occasional sweet chestnut. As you approach the next kissing gate, there is a park bench between two lime trees. A good spot for a picnic or simply to sit and take in the view.

The footpath used to go through a rock tunnel at this point but the roof became unstable and the tunnel has been closed. This is a pity

Warnscale Beck and Buttermere *(Bill Stainton)*

as it was a great hit with children of all ages. The route now climbs steeply over the tunnel, starting at the rock outcrop just to the left of the tunnel entrance.

The first part of the climb is a scramble but once you are at the top it becomes a delightful walk through woodland again. Look out for a spectacular outcrop of rock in the trees above you, on your left, as you start to descend.

Once back on the lake shore path, go through another kissing gate (romantically inclined couples can take up to four days to complete this walk) and onto a tree-lined beach. Well, don't expect sand castles – it is a shingle beach. The lake will eventually be full of flat stones skipped across the water at this point. The temptation is tremendous.

Leaving the trees behind, follow the path through another kissing gate and past a small plantation of firs. There is a dramatic view of Fleetwith Pike ahead and on the opposite shore you can see Comb Beck tumbling down from High Crag.

When you pass a sign for 'Permissive Lake Shore Path', bear right and keep to the shore. After another gate (I'll let you guess which sort), the path is running just below the main road, so take care of

Looking across Buttermere to Fleetwith Pike *(Bill Stainton)*

dogs and children at this point. Another 300m and the path joins the road, beside another beach.

The next 600m are along the road. Keep close to the walls and watch out for traffic. After a few minutes, you come to the road bridge over Gatesgarth Beck. Once over the bridge, turn right, along the path by Gatesgarth Farm. (The car park opposite the farm is more expensive than at Buttermere village, but does offer a useful alternative starting point if Buttermere is full. It also has the advantage of a permanently stationed ice cream van in the school holidays.)

The path works around the farm to a cluster of gates. Go through the small gate signed 'Lake Shore Path' and follow the path across the fields. You get an amazing view to your left of Fleetwith Pike, Hay Stacks and Warnscale Beck. This part of the valley is a popular starting point for the climb to Great Gable and Scafell Pike.

Once through the gate on the far side of the fields, the path forks. Unless you've an overriding urge to include Ennerdale on the itinerary, turn right (signed 'Public Bridleway: Buttermere').

You cross a beck as it dashes through the rocks, then leave the bridleway to go right, along the lake shore path. After ten minutes walking, you enter Burtness Wood. Like most of this area, the wood is owned and managed by the National Trust.

A short distance into the woods, the path forks. Go right and you keep to the shore for a view of the woods at Hassness, on the far shore. Once again, there are a few conveniently placed benches along the shore.

The path rejoins the main track and plunges through an intriguing swathe of beech trees, which feels out of place amongst all the fir. You walk through the woods towards the foot of the lake, eventually arriving at a fence and a pair of gates. The path left climbs to Red Pike and Ennerdale. Keep right, through the wooden gate and across the pair of wooden bridges, which take you over Sourmilk Gill and Buttermere Dubs. Again, there is an excellent view of Fleetwith at the head of the lake.

Once over the second bridge, you have a choice. If you head straight, you leave the field to join a farm lane which eventually takes you back to the Bridge Hotel and the centre of the village. This is the way most people come out from the village. In recent years, a more attractive alternative has been negotiated which goes along the edge of the lake and across the fields. This is the route we take but bear in mind that this route is closed during lambing time.

Go right from the bridge and all dogs immediately on leads, please, as you may encounter livestock. Following the shore means you get the benefit of that terrific view of the mountains at the far end of the lake. Amateur photographers should take note that there are plenty of overhanging branches along here to frame that prize-winning photograph.

The path crosses five fields, keeping to the shore throughout. Each field boundary has a stile and there are one or two with wire flaps for dogs. Finally, you leave the fifth field, cross a small beck and the path goes left, up the field to join the outgoing path. Back into the village for a tea at one of the hotels.

NOTES

[1] The name Buttermere is usually interpreted as the lake by the diary pastures, although there is an older derivation from Buthar, the Norse owner of the lake. It is 2km (1.24 miles) long, less than 28m (94ft) deep and is home to the char, a comparatively rare Lakeland fish. The lake is owned by the National Trust. Buttermere and Crummock Water were once one large lake, formed by the last Ice Age. Debris washed into the valley formed the delta which now separates them.

Buttermere was a well-known beauty spot in Wordsworth's day and was once the scene of a national scandal. In 1792, Captain Joseph Budworth published a guide book to the area, 'A Fortnight's Ramble in the Lakes'. He went into raptures over the innocent beauty of one Mary Robinson, the inn keeper's 15-year-old daughter at the Fish Inn. He sang her praises at such embarrassing length that he toned down his remarks in subsequent editions for fear of attracting unsavoury characters. (Oddly enough, the habit of mentioning attractive locals in guide books has not continued to the present day.)

In 1802, the Honourable Alexander Augustus Hope, MP for Linlithgow, arrived in the area, was a big hit with the locals and within six weeks had married Mary Robinson at Lorton church. Samuel Taylor Coleridge was living at Keswick at the time and was a correspondent for the London Morning Post. He duly wrote up the romantic courtship, emphasising what a lucky catch the inn keeper's daughter had made. It began to look less lucky, however, when Charles Hope reported that his brother was at the time enjoying a holiday in Europe. The bogus MP was revealed to be James Hatfield, a noted swindler and bigamist. There was an immense outcry, not least among the local gentry who had been so keen to suck up to him.

As soon as Hatfield and his new wife arrived back from their honeymoon in Scotland, he was arrested. He used his talents to persuade the local constabulary to allow him to go fishing for the day and, not surprisingly, did not come back. He escaped over the fells to Ravenglass and caught a ship to Liverpool (Ravenglass was a major port at the time). He was arrested several weeks later in Wales, tried in Carlisle and hanged (not for bigamy but for defrauding the post office by franking his letters as an MP). The severity of the sentence was in part due to the national sympathy for Mary, whipped up by the press. Mary remarried in 1808 and died in 1837. She is buried in Caldbeck churchyard.

The story was immediately taken up by writers and playwrights. Wordsworth praised Mary's virtue in his epic poem, 'The Prelude'. The latest contribution to the genre is Melvyn Bragg's 'The Maid of Buttermer'e, published in 1987. The George Shelbourn who appears in Mr Bragg's novel is a distant relation of mine.

WATERSIDE WALKS IN THE LAKE DISTRICT

18

LOWESWATER

Located in the north west corner of the Lake District National
Park, Loweswater is an excellent place to head when the
central lakes have become too busy. It lies in splendid
seclusion, out beyond the further reaches of Crummock
Water and Buttermere. The valley is peaceful and rural and
the lake tends to be appreciated more by locals than visitors.
This is a superb walk along a tree-lined shore, with a short
climb to the added bonus of a view to the Solway Firth and
Scotland.

Distance and terrain: 6.5km (4 miles). Very easy walking for
the most part with a short steep climb up the lane at Miresyke.

Parking: National Trust pay-and-display car park at Maggie's
Bridge (GR135210). To find this, head north west along the
minor road between Loweswater village and Mockerkin and turn
left just after the old Loweswater school (signposted PUBLIC
BRIDLEWAY). It is 100m beyond the turning right to
Thackthwaite. Alternative parking is available along the road
beside Loweswater or – if you don't mind the walk back along
the road – at the National Trust Lanthwaite Wood car park.

L eaving the car park, continue down the lane and through the gate
(signed 'Watergate Farm, Watergate Cottage and Holme Wood
Bothy'). Cross over Dub Beck and follow the track through pleasant,
open farm land.

When you reach the first cattle grid, ignore the stile on the right
which tempts you to the foot of the lake. Continue along the track
and enjoy the view of Darling Fell on the far side of the lake.

The track leads you across the fields, approaching a group of
houses Holme Wood and Watergate House). 50m from the house,
the path goes right, across the field, to a stile and farm gate at the

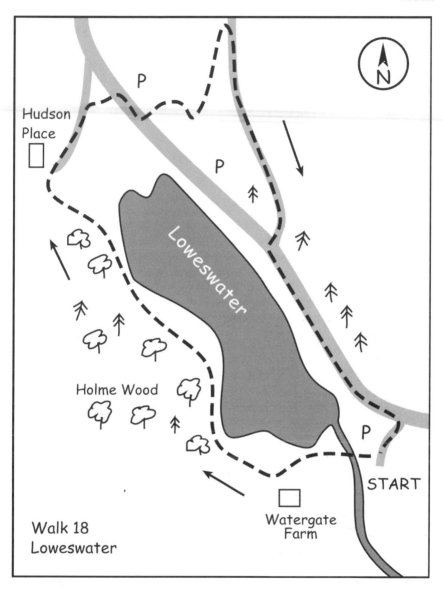

Walk 18
Loweswater

entrance to Holme Wood. Over the stile and there is a park bench on
your right, if you fancy a stop to take in the view of Loweswater [1].
This is a lovely wooded track, reeds and lapping water by your side
as you follow the path through the woods. It is very peaceful. At various points you get good views of Loweswater Fell and Whiteside.

From deciduous woodland, you enter an area predominantly conifer. After a few metres, you cross a small beck (via two wooden railway sleepers) and the path forks.

The main track goes straight ahead but, instead, follow the path right, to keep to the lake shore, and you come to a stone hut in the woods, beside the lake. This is Holme Wood Bothy, owned by the National Trust. What a brilliant place to camp, even if you do spend all your time watching out for the Seven Dwarves.

Continue along the path, keeping to the lake shore whenever it forks. You eventually come to a fence. Follow the path left and you rejoin the forestry track and turn right to a farm gate and stile. Cross into the field and continue along the path. This is a reedy lakeside field (look out for pied flycatcher, grebes and, in winter, goldeneye.) This is a very pretty view, particularly back along the lake, with little sign of human cultivation.

You reach another gate, which takes you onto a narrow track between two stone walls and, after a couple of minutes walking, to Hudson Place, an eighteenth century farmhouse. Go right and follow the tarmac lane downhill.

Once past the farmhouse, ignore the path indicated left and continue down the lane (signed 'Waterend'). As the lane levels off, look out for a stile in the wire fence on your right (next to the metal farm gate). Cross the stile and go straight across the field towards a stile in the fence on the far side. You cross a wooden causeway over the marsh.

Over the stile (note the dog stile next to it, greatly appreciated by chief researcher), over a small beck and then bear right to another stile in the hedge on your right. Once over, the path goes left, up the field to a kissing gate and the main road.

Turn right and you could follow the road back to the track which leads to the National Trust car park. However, it is nearly 2km and a bit of drag (especially for chief researchers), so there is an alternative route. Just past the telephone box, there is a lane on the left, signed 'Public Bridleway to Mossergate'. Go up this steep, narrow lane (look out for a farm gate and good views) until it peters out into a rough track at a T-junction.

Go left, then immediately right, up another rough lane, signed 'Path to Mosserfell'. This section is steep and rough underfoot. It takes you up to a farm gate and once through you are in a fell side field with increasingly good views back over the lake. As you get to

Across Loweswater to, from left: Whiteside, Grasmoor and Whiteless Pike *(Bill Stainton)*

the next farm gate, that distant hazy patch you may be able to see ahead of you is the sea at the Solway Firth and beyond it, Scotland.

Through the gate and on uphill to the next one. Over the stile and turn sharp right, heading back in the direction of Loweswater. Once round a corner, there are lovely views of the lake.

As you can tell from the grass growing down the centre, this tarmac lane is not heavily used. Ignore the footpath left to Foulsyke and continue down the lane, into a small wood and onto the main road again. Go left along the road (and look out for the neat weather vane on Crabtree Beck House). Despite the proximity of the lake, there is no real lake shore footpath along here. Continue along the road and after about a mile, you come to the lane (signed 'Public Bridleway') to the National Trust car park. (If you reach the school house, you've walked too far.) Turn right, down the lane and back to the car park.

NOTES

[1] Loweswater means 'the leafy lake', derived from the Old Norse Laufs-saer-vatn. It is owned by the National Trust and is only 2.4km (1.5 miles) long and 0.8km (0.5 miles) wide. At its deepest point it is 18.2m (60ft) and it is unique among the sixteen lakes in that water leaving it flows towards the centre of the Lake District.

19

THIRLMERE & HARROP TARN

Until the early 1980s, access to the shore of Thirlmere was severely restricted. A reservoir for over 100 years, the Victorian filtration plant couldn't cope with hordes of grubby tourist splashing about in the water. After considerable improvement works and negotiation from the Lake District National Park Authority, the lake was opened to the public for the first time. There is now a footpath along the entire western shore. The water is very clear and pure and the comparative lack of traffic makes this a delightful area to explore. This route combines a walk along the shore with a climb to a lovely, secluded tarn in the trees above Birk Crag.

Distance and terrain: 6.5km (4 miles) for the extended walk. 3.75km (2.4 miles) if starting and finishing at Dobgill car park. The walk along the lake shore is level, easy walking. The climb alongside Dob Gill is steep, though fairly secure underfoot. The descent is long and gentle.

Parking: North West Water car park at Steel End (GR 321129), at the south west corner of the lake. Alternatively, to do the shorter route, park at Dobgill car park (GR 316139), 1.2km further along the road.

There are two starting points for this walk. Beginning at Steel End car park and walking along the shore to Dob Gill gives you a chance to warm up and enjoy the views before the stiff climb to Harrop Tarn. However, you have to retrace this 1.35km section at the end of the walk so the alternative is to begin at the Dobgill car park. This car park has the benefit of a loo block so you might consider it a more civilised point to end the walk. The choice is yours!

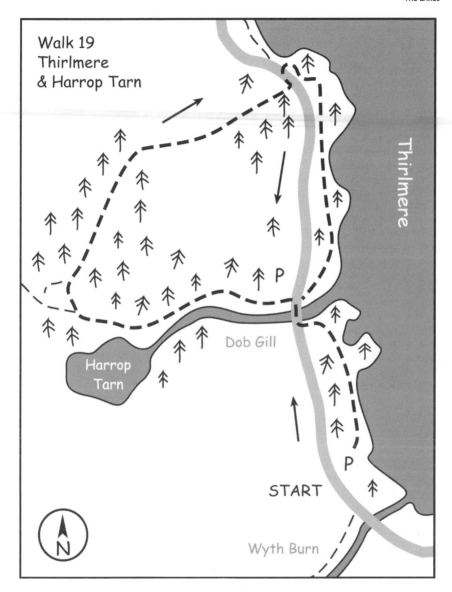

Walk 19
Thirlmere
& Harrop Tarn

Thirlmere

P

Harrop
Tarn

Dob Gill

P

START

Wyth Burn

N

FROM STEEL END CAR PARK

Leave the car park via the kissing gate and you are immediately on a forestry path which winds through the trees, alongside Wyth Burn (a curiously Scottish-sounding name for a Lakeland beck). After

50m or so you leave the woods and have a magnificent view of the western flanks of Helvellyn, with Whelpside Gill, the white streak directly in front of you.

The path is very clear and winds across the open grass and marsh, crossing a number of smaller becks before heading into the trees again. Keeping to the edge of the forest, you can see Wythburn church on the far side of the valley, directly next to the road. The path bends back into the woods, over three boardwalks and then brings you to the shore of Thirlmere [1].

You pass a marker post and then 30m beyond that the path winds to the edge of the wood to give you a clear view along the length of the lake to the easily recognisable shape of Blencathra. The shape gives the mountain its other, more prosaic name of Saddleback.

Ignore the erosion path into the trees and keep to the edge of the wood, crossing rocks and stones for 60m or so before coming to a wire fence. Through the gate and onto a rock outcrop for another good view of the lake.

The path then goes back into the woods, over a 30m boardwalk and then begins to get boggy. The route follows the line of the overhead telegraph wires, bringing you alongside a wire fence. Follow the fence line to a forestry track and turn right, towards the lake. The track disappears very quickly and the path swings off left, along the fence and remains of a dry stone wall. When you reach a marker post at a gap between two walls, turn left and head up the hill to the gate in the stone wall. (Alternatively, divert to the right for a look at Dob Gill.)

The gate brings you out onto the road at Dobgill Bridge. Follow the road north and 100m beyond the bridge, cross over into Dobgill car park. (In case you were wondering, it is a common but confusing Lakeland habit to contract a name like Dob Gill into one word when car park or force is added.)

FROM DOBGILL CAR PARK

At the top, left corner of the car park is a short flight of wooden steps which leads you up into the trees and is signed 'Harrop Tarn'.

Climbing uphill you encounter what must be the tallest kissing gate in the Lake District. This is not for amorous giraffes but is designed to keep red deer away from the road. When I walked this route one November, there was a sign on the gate which warned: Do

Thirlmere with Blencathra beyond *(Bill Stainton)*

not wander from the path, stalking in progress. Climbing uphill through an early winter snowfall, I thought this lent the forest an added air of danger and excitement. I didn't see anyone apart from a couple of fell-walkers also nervously peering through the trees so perhaps it was a ruse to prevent ramblers crashing about through the woods.

Go through the kissing gate and up a stone path to begin climbing steeply through the trees. The path zigzags below an impressive rocky knoll, then winds round the side of the knoll to reach Dob Gill and an impressive cascade and pool.

Continue past the waterfall into the dark conifer forest. After a few minutes gentle uphill walking, you come in sight of Harrop Tarn [2]. This is a very pretty, reedy tarn, surrounded by conifers and overlooked by Tarn Crags on the far side. You join a forest track and there is a sign immediately in front of you. Go right (the WHITE ROUTE) and after 100m or so the conifers give way to a short section of birch trees. Harrop Tarn is not exactly huge and after another 100m, you have passed the head of it.

The track takes you gently uphill through the forest, accompanied by a gurgling beck on your left. After crossing three small streams, you come to a path (signed 'Watendlath') which disappears into the trees on your left and would seem to offer all sorts of exciting possibilities. This, however, is for real mountain men (and women) so for the rest of us, keep following the track to a T-junction. Go right, alongside another small beck which comes crashing down a small outcrop of rock on your left. Surrounded by larch, this is very pretty in autumn.

After another 100m, you come to another junction and a superb view over the trees to the summit of Helvellyn. A logging track swings right. If no stalkers are about, it is worth a swift diversion to the top of Swithin Crag, the rocky knoll in front of you, just above the curve of the logging track. From the crag you get a terrific panorama of Thirlmere valley.

Continue along the main track, past a track joining from the left, and you begin the slow descent. You lose sight of Helvellyn as the trees close in around you and the hill side drops away steeply on the right.

The tracks drops to a gate. Note the extension bolted onto the top of the gate to keep in the deer. Once through, you have another good view of Helvellyn and Thirlmere. Cragsteads Gill crashes down the rocks on your left, passing under the track.

The official white route swings right here, going down a narrow path along the edge of the forestry plantation. This makes a steep descent to the road and a walk back to Dobgill car park. Ignore it and continue down the track across open fell, enjoying the views.

The track zigzags down to another gate and then you are back in the forest again. Eventually you come down to the road.

Go left along the road for 125m and you come to a cutting, where the road has been blasted through an outcrop of rock. There are three gates on the right-hand side of the road. Were going through the first (signed 'Dobgill') but first, go to the far side of the outcrop and through the gate which leads you to the top of the rock and the view. This is Hause Point and until the early 1980s, this was one of the few access points to Thirlmere. All 20m of it. How things have improved since then.

Go through the gate ('Dobgill') and enjoy the lovely, wooded shore walk. After 1km of blissful, easy walking, you pass a rocky promontory. I defy any reader to resist the temptation to go to the end of this and look at the view.

Shortly after this, the path begins to wind inland, skirting the end of Dob Gill as it joins Thirlmere. Up the marshy field to a kissing gate and you rejoin the road opposite Dobgill car park. If you've parked here, congratulate yourself and go and get out of muddy boots. If your car is at Steel End, turn left along the road and retrace the outgoing route to the start of the walk.

NOTES

[1] In the 1870s, Manchester Corporation Water Works began campaigning to buy two small lakes, Leathes Water and Brackmere, in order to dam them and provide a new reservoir for Manchester. There was tremendous local and national opposition, objectors fearing that the beauty of the area would be ruined forever. A Thirlmere Defence Association was formed, questions were asked in Parliament and the local landowner, Thomas Leathe of Dalehead Hall, was so adamant that he would never sell the land that surveys had to be conducted by the Corporation in secret. But when Leathe died, his son sold the required 11,000 acres, the Thirlmere Bill was passed in 1879 and work began in 1886.

The 30m (98ft) high dam raised the water level by 16.5m (54ft), flooding two small villages and creating the lake we see today. The first water arrived in Manchester in October 1894, carried there by a 153km (95 mile) gravity-fed aqueduct. A marvel of Victorian engineering, the aqueduct is over 2m in diameter and tunnels 460m (1500ft) through Dunmail Raise, which alone took four years to dig.

Interestingly, one of the chief objectors to the creation of Thirlmere was John Ruskin, who lived at Coniston at the time. The public outcry against the scheme helped establish the climate which gave birth to the National Trust, one year after the aqueduct was opened.

The name 'Thirlmere' means a narrow stretch of water. The lake is 5.6km (3.5 miles) long, 0.8km (0.5 mile) wide and 48m (158ft) deep.

[2] Harrop Tarn is only around 4.5m deep and is a remnant of the Ice Age, dammed by a glacial moraine. It is gradually silting up, so do the walk whilst it is still here.

20

RYDAL WATER & GRASMERE

Rydal Water and Grasmere are the classic English lakes. This walk begins with a climb to Loughrigg Terrace for a wonderful view of Grasmere, before dropping to the lake shore and coming back along the River Rothay and the shores of Rydal Water. The route out takes best advantage of the views and you are accompanied by water all the way back.

Distance and terrain: 7km (5 miles). Easy walking, some uphill to begin and then a gentle stroll back.

Parking: National Park car park at Pelter Bridge, just off the A591, south of Rydal Hall (GR 365060). Limited parking.

The lane heads away from the bridge (turning left out of the car park), past Cote How Guest House, a pair of Lakeland stone cottages and a short terrace. The tarmac lane ends at a wooden farm gate. Go through the gap alongside and continue along the rough track to another gate. As you go through the gate, the bridleway is signed right, along the shore, but our route continues straight on, along the upper path. Pause at the wooden bench and take in the view of Rydal Water [1], with its two small islands.

The track leads you past the lake and alongside a stone wall, losing the view behind the trees. Follow the fence line and you cross a small beck and climb to the first of Rydal caves. These are actually old slate quarries. You can just about scramble into the first of these, but it is wet and dark, so there is not a great deal to see. Getting down from the cave will seem a lot more difficult than the 2m climb up.

Continue along the path and climb up the side of a slate tip to a small plateau and the second of the caves. This is much bigger – whole choirs from Charlotte Mason College have been known to sing Christmas carols in here. The acoustics are perhaps not on a par

The view from the larger of the Rydal caves *(Bill Stainton)*

with the Albert Hall, but the sight of the cave lit up with headtorches and candles makes for a memorable concert.

The route continues past the cave and up a slight rise to a good viewpoint, taking in Rydal Water on your right, looking across the lake to Nab Scar and, below it, Nab Cottage [2]. Leaving this vantage point, head along the path, winding around the side of Loughrigg (ignore the path beaten through the bracken on the right). The path goes to the left of a small conifer plantation and then forks. Go left again, on the narrower path, climbing steeply onto Loughrigg Terrace.

Pig Lake [3] is very pretty, surrounded by high fells, with an island almost exactly in the centre. On a still, Autumn morning, the setting is perfect. The lake and island are owned by the National Trust and the islands stone barn used to be used for sheltering sheep (which were brought across in flat bottomed boats). The lake is 1.6km (1 mile) long, 0.8km (0.5 miles) wide, and around 22m (75ft) deep.

This is a superb viewpoint which just gets better and better. Turn left and as you walk along the terrace you can see Grasmere coming into view, above it the distinctive cone of Helm Crag and, to the right, Dunmail Raise [4] is the U-shaped saddle between Helm Crag and Fairfield. The path drops to cross a small beck and then brings you to a pair of gates. Go through the kissing gate and turn immediately right, through another kissing gate (signed 'Grasmere'). This takes you into Deerbolts Wood, once part of High Close estate. (High Close House is now a youth hostel.)

The path slopes gently downhill, taking you through delightful mixed woodland, full of traditional English trees, such as beech, sycamore and larch. After a few minutes steady descent, you arrive at the National Trust warden's cottage. Turn sharp right (signed 'Lake, White Moss & Rydal') and follow the path down through the woods to Grasmere shore.

As you approach the stone wall at the boundary of the woods, there are two gates. Go through the left-hand one, on the shore, and enjoy a paddle along the shingle beach. There is a lovely view of the valley and the grassy bank is an ideal picnic spot.

Follow the shore along to the wooden footbridge, just past the weir. Do not cross the bridge, but continue along the path alongside the river, heading downstream towards another wood. This is a nice, clear river. Keep an eye out for kingfishers, tigers and wild elephants along here. You probably wont see any but I like to encourage my readers to keep an open mind.

After four or five minutes, you go through a kissing gate and into another wood. Through another kissing gate and the path climbs above the river. The rush of water is very encouraging and drowns out most of the surrounding sound, apart from the occasional fighter plane. Keep to the river bank and the path brings you to another footbridge.

There are two reasons why you might want to cross here; the public loos and the ice cream van which inevitably stands in White Moss car park, on the far side of the A591.

If neither of these strike you as particularly compelling, turn right here and follow the path away from the bridge. (As a third alternative, you could continue straight on at the bridge and follow a path along a wetland conservation area walkway. If so, keep dogs on leads, particularly in spring time when you might disturb nesting waterfowl.)

The path heads uphill, signed 'Loughrigg Terrace', and brings you to yet another kissing gate in a stone wall. Go through, turn left

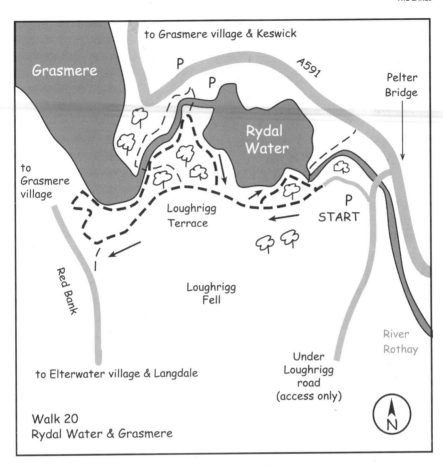

to Grasmere village & Keswick

Grasmere

P

P

A591

Pelter
Bridge

Rydal
Water

to
Grasmere
village

Loughrigg
Terrace

P
START

Red Bank

Loughrigg
Fell

River
Rothay

to Elterwater village & Langdale

Under
Loughrigg
road
(access only)

N

Walk 20
Rydal Water & Grasmere

and keep to the stone wall. The path eventually brings you back to Rydal Water, dropping down to the lake shore and a very pleasant stroll along the waters edge.

Eventually you run out of beach and come to yet another kissing gate in a stone wall. Go through and follow the path through Rydal Woods. You leave the woods via a nice old iron kissing gate and find yourself in a field at the foot of Rydal Water. Follow the clear path across the field and alongside the Rothay again (the Rothay effectively links Grasmere and Rydal to Windermere). After a couple of minutes you approach a footbridge, which leads up to the road. Do not cross the bridge but turn right and follow the less distinct path up the field to another kissing gate. Once through you are in the woods again. Continue uphill, up twelve steps and through a final gate to emerge on the tarmac lane from Pelter Bridge. Turn right and retrace your steps to the start.

NOTES

[1] Rydal Water is a pretty little lake, despite the proximity of the A591 along its eastern shore. Once known as Rothaymere (after the river which flows through) it is less than 1.2km (0.75 miles) long by 0.4km (0.25 miles) and only around 16m (55ft) deep. It is very popular for swimming and, being comparatively shallow, it doesn't take too long to warm up in summer.

[2] In an area seething with Wordsworth associations, it should come as no surprise to discover that Nab Cottage also has literary connections. Built as a farm house in 1702, it was once the home of Thomas De Quincey, famous for his book 'Confessions of an English Opium Eater'. He first came to Grasmere in 1807, specifically to visit his great hero, Wordsworth. He stayed with the family at Dove Cottage for several months and when they moved out to Allan Bank, Thomas took over the tenancy. Whilst living at Dove Cottage, he courted Margaret Simpson, whose father owned Nab Farm (as it was called then). Wordsworth thought De Quincey should not marry such a lowborn woman and wrote complaining letters to De Quincey's mum. It didn't work; Thomas married Margaret in 1817. In 1829, he bought the farm from her father and moved in. He kept on Dove Cottage for another ten years to store his vast library of books. Nab Cottage is now a guest house.

I have to admit to a great liking for De Quincey and when working at Dove Cottage as a guide, used to vary the routine with occasional De Quincey tours. His 'Recollections of the Lake Poets' (Penguin) brings the Wordsworth's Grasmere years vividly to life and should be required reading before visiting Dove Cottage.

[3] There are several variations on the origin of the name Grasmere. The popular one is that it is Old English for the lake with the grassy shore. More likely it derives from the Viking settlers, who kept pigs in the surrounding woods; they would have known it as Grismere, 'griss' being Scandinavian for pig.

[4] Dunmail Raise is named after the last King of Cumberland, supposedly buried here after his defeat by the Saxon king, Edmund, in 945 AD. In fact, he is rumoured to have died on a pilgrimage to Rome nearly 30 years later. The Raise marks the boundary between the old counties of Cumberland and Westmorland.

You pass a number of wooden seats along the terrace. At the fourth, pause for a rest and enjoy the view. (If the seat has been bagged by someone else clutching a copy of this book, tell them there is a better view over the page and push them off.)

Just visible over Dunmail is the summit of Blencathra. Follow the view round to the left and the dull yellow building below Helm Crag is Allan Bank, one of Wordsworth's three Grasmere homes.

Allan Bank is highly visible from most of the surrounding fells. It was this fact that led Wordsworth to describe it as 'a temple of abomination' when it was built in 1805 by a Liverpool merchant named Crump. Three years later, when the Wordsworth's had outgrown the accommodation at Dove Cottage, Allan Bank proved the only house in Grasmere large enough to take them all. Wordsworth lived there for nearly three years, but the chimneys smoked and the rooms were cold, so as soon as the rectory became available, the family moved out. The house is now owned by the National Trust and rented privately.

21

ELTERWATER

Elterwater is an old Norse name meaning the lake of the swans. It is not as dramatic as some of the major lakes but can be the focus of several superb low level walks. This is a walk across gentle countryside which includes two small waterfalls, Colwith Force and Skelwith Force.

Distance and terrain: 8.25km (5 miles). Easy walking, some across fields which will probably be muddy in winter. Very little climbing and a number of shortcut points.

Parking: National Trust car park in the village centre. Get there early as it fills very quickly, largely due to the immense popularity of the nearby Britannia Inn.

On the principle that the boring bits should be eliminated first, from the car park, head out to the road and turn left, over the road bridge. Follow the road, taking the opportunity to enjoy the views across the fields to the lake. This is a relatively quiet stretch of country lane but there are a number of blind corners, so take care. You'll be on the road for about a kilometre.

Beyond the youth hostel (originally a seventeenth century farmhouse) and Elterwater Country House Hotel (the latter now owned by the Langdale timeshare complex), there is a long, uninhabited stretch before passing the entrance to a house on your left. 50m or so beyond that, there is a sign on your right for Fletchers Wood, a National Trust owned woodland. Go over the stile, and a path leads you through the trees, past oak, birch and the occasional larch.

The path leads to another stile. Cross and continue up a field – keeping the stone wall to your right – to a vehicle track. Go right, along the track. Go through the first white farm gate, just past a barn, and continue along the track until you come in sight of a white house on your right. Look out for a stile and footpath sign in the

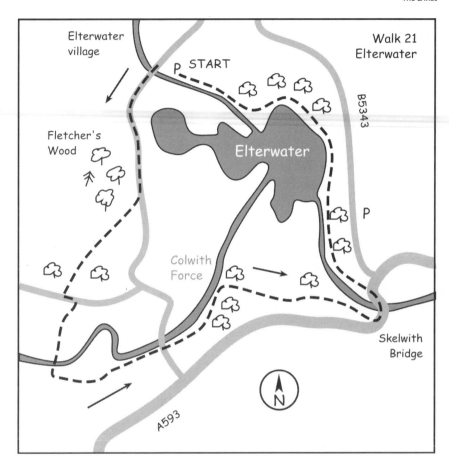

Elterwater village

Walk 21
Elterwater

P START

Fletcher's Wood

Elterwater

B5343

Colwith Force

Skelwith Bridge

N

A593

stone wall on your left. Cross the stile, into a field, and follow the wall on your right. This little diversion takes you around the house and grounds. Keep to the field boundary and you are on the right route. At the corner of the field, cross the stone wall via the next stile and then bear slightly right, through a gap in a stone wall.

The route goes left here but before you head downhill, go across to the farm gate in the wall in front of you for an excellent view of Wetherlam. Then head down the field. The path is indistinct, so keep to the wall on your right and you come to a wooden farm gate in the corner of the field. The way this gate is hinged into the wall is pretty interesting, using the stone wall as part of the hinge.

Go through the gate and turn right, then, as soon as you cross the beck, bear left and follow the beck downhill for 20m. The path then bears away from the beck, across the field towards a neat black and white farmhouse.

The path forks left just before the farm, taking you to a stile in the wire fence. Once over, you are on a gravelled drive next to Irving Howe farm. Go left, down the drive to the road.

Turn right along the road and you are heading into Little Langdale. There is a brilliant view of Wetherlam across the fields to your left. The road along here is very narrow, so watch out for cars. Especially in summer, visitors seem to find the stone walls strangely intimidating and tend to drive in the middle of the road. Watch out for the sign on the gate of Green Bank Cottage ('Never mind the dog, beware the owner').

You walk past a terrace of houses and, just after Lang Parrock, look out for a narrow kissing gate on the left, just by the parking space for Greenbank Terrace. The gate has a sign which reads Please keep in single file, growing crop, herb-rich meadow. Before you go through, bear in mind that if any members of the party feel tired and thirsty, the Three Shires Inn is just a few hundred metres further along the road.

Go through the gate and head straight across the field to the far corner (the footpath is very clear across the field). Cross the narrow wooden footbridge over Greenburn Beck and then bear right, then follow the path towards the white farmhouse at the top of the field. The path goes between a wire fence and stone wall, past the front of Stang End farm and out onto a tarmac lane.

Go left and immediately come to a sign and a fork in the road. Go left, signed 'Colwith and Skelwith'. This is an extremely narrow lane, so if a car approaches be prepared to leap nimbly into the adjoining field. As you stroll along, enjoy the views left across the field to the Three Shires Inn. It is too late to go back to it now.

In less than ten minutes, you should come to High Park farm. There is a public footpath through the farmyard to a wooden gate which takes you into a field. The path goes straight across to the kissing gate in the wall ahead. Once beyond the wall, turn left and follow the path to another gate which takes you into the woods. The path forks immediately. Go left on the path, signed 'Colwith Force', down through the trees, towards the sound of rushing water.

At last, you come to a wide river which winds through the wood.

Elterwater and the Langdale Pikes *(Bill Stainton)*

The path follows the river downstream and after a few minutes brings you to a superb view of Colwith Force, a 21m cascade, sheltered by trees in a rocky ravine.

Continue downstream, following the clearly defined path through the trees. Eventually you come to a road. Colwith Bridge, on your left, stands on the old county boundary between Lancashire and Westmorland. You, however, should go right along the road for 100m or so.

Just past a lay-by and bridge, there is a stile in the stone wall on your left, signed 'Skelwith Bridge'. Go through and follow the path across the field to the woods to rejoin the river. Just inside the wood, cross the stile and climb steeply up the bank. From the vast hole excavated by the chief researcher at this point, I think we can safely assume there are moles in this wood.

You climb to a wire fence and then follow the path left along the fence to a stile. This takes you into a field and gives you a view of Loughrigg. Go across the field and through a metal kissing gate beside Low Park house. Straight over the drive and over a narrow stile and down a path between two walls. This takes you to another stile and across another field to yet another stile.

You now come to Park Farm. Look for the yellow marker arrow on the side of one of the stone barns and the route goes between the buildings and down a vehicle track. Go past the static caravans and through the gate and keep to the vehicle track, past a small wood on your right.

At the end of the track, on the far side of the field, you come to Park House and the centre of some controversy. At the time of writing, although the right of way goes through the grounds of Park House, there is a permissive path which diverts you around the garden. Be kind and follow this path: the owners of Park House have enough people going through their garden without us adding to their number. The track then takes you past a house called Tiplog and through a gateway. 20m beyond the gate, watch out for a marker post on your left and take the path left, across the open field.

Another kissing gate takes you into Bridge Howe Coppice and towards a wooden bungalow. Fork right, around the bungalow to a wooden kissing gate. This takes you through and onto the tarmac road. Go left and follow the road round the corner and over the bridge. Just past is the entrance to Kirkstone Slate Gallery [1] and the car park. The route goes through the gallery car park (signed 'Public Footpath to Elterwater'). Where the tarmac drive forks, by Riverside Cottage, go right, through the slate works and into the trees beside the River Brathay. You have now left behind all further roads and dogs, children and elderly relatives can be safely unleashed.

The path leads upstream, past the small but vigorous waterfall [2]. For a good look at this, go over the two iron footbridges built on the rocks in the middle of the river. The path brings you to a kissing gate and into another field. Go straight across, heading to the left of the clump of trees ahead of you. This is a nice, wide expanse after all the woods and narrow lanes. As you follow the broad river, the view of the Langdale Pikes opens up in front of you.

Beyond the trees, go through a farm gate and keep following the river. As you approach the next gate and the wood, you reach the foot of Elterwater [3] and a classic view across the water to the mountains.

Into the woods and follow the footpath around the edge of the lake. This is a lovely wood in spring when it is a mass of bluebells. The path winds round to the left, following a wire fence as you lose sight of the lake and crossing a wooden footbridge. You are now beside the river once more and a very easy, level path takes you straight back to the car park at Elterwater village.

NOTES

[1] Kirkstone Slate Gallery has a superb cafe and shop and the slate works behind works the local green-blue slate. The slate is exported around the world and in the gallery you can buy anything from a slate ashtray to a slate fireplace. The Gallery has recently been renamed the Touchstone Gallery, but it'll be years before locals and writers get used to calling it that.

[2] At only 6m high, this isn't the most impressive waterfall in the Lake District, though it does lay claim to having the highest volume of falling water, due to the large catchment area of surrounding fells.

[3] Elterwater is the smallest of the 16 lakes, less than 1km long and only 15m (48ft) at its deepest point.

22

ULLSWATER

Ullswater is arguably the most attractive of the sixteen lakes. The second longest, it lies in the heart of dramatic scenery and does not suffer the noise and visitor pressure which plague Windermere. The south east shore has no roads, no traffic and very little habitation. You are in wild and lovely countryside with the prospect of a steamer trip back to the car.

Although this route is commonly walked in reverse, I'm a firm believer in dispensing with the slog along the road as quickly as possible. However, this does mean you should give yourself plenty of time to do the walk and don't aim for last steamer of the day. If you miss it, you will have a long walk back.

Distance and terrain: 10.5km (6.5 miles). Level walking for most of the way with some short uphill sections.

Parking: Ullswater steamers car park at Glenridding (south side of the village on the A592). GR 390169.

Once you've armed yourself with a timetable from the steamer ticket office, head back across the car park and go through the farm gate by the road entrance. This leads into the field and a nice stroll along the lake shore. It brings you out at the A592 next to a snack bar (very convenient). Before crossing, if you look left along the road you can see St Patrick's Well in the stone wall.

Cross the road to a set of steps directly opposite (signed 'Permissive Path to Patterdale') and follow the path left, parallel to the road. This avoids a few hundred metres of pavement. You come back to the road at the entrance to Patterdale Hall estate. Cross again and there is another short section of off-road footpath before you are

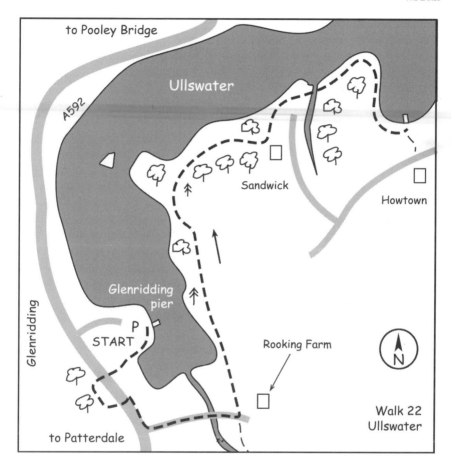

to Pooley Bridge

Ullswater

A592

Sandwick

Howtown

Glenridding
pier

Glenridding

P

START

Rooking Farm

N

to Patterdale

Walk 22
Ullswater

forced to walk along the pavement, heading in the direction of Patterdale village [1]. After 350m, you past St Patrick's church and the rectory and come to a turning on your left, beside a stone built hall (look for the Club Alpine Swiss sign, dating from 1863). Turn left down the lane, signed 'To Howtown & Boredale'.

The track leads you across the fields to Side Farm, which, if you are already flagging, sells ice creams. Go into the farm yard and at the top, by the shop, turn left, signed 'Howtown & Sandwick'. Go through the farm gate and follow the track.

There is a good view left of Glenridding and Helvellyn, although photographers may grumble about the ugly iron farm shed in the middle distance. From this point you can see Dollywagon Pike, High

Crag and the western tip of St Sunday Crag. You are on a very easy track, the fell side rising up on your right and an increasingly good view of Ullswater [2] on your left. You occasionally see red squirrels in the trees along here and you might encounter groups of pony trekkers from Side Farm.

After you've been walking for fifty minutes or so, the wall starts to drop away to your left and you climb a short rise. Suddenly you've got the most magnificent view of the lake, Norfolk Island in the centre, green rolling fells on the far side, a mighty Scots pine on your left – an ideal spot for a picnic. The track narrows to a path and this is a lovely part of the walk. The view of the lake is a constant companion. On the far shore you may be able to spot a grey, square tower rising above the trees. This is Lyulph's Tower [3], in Gowbarrow Park, just east of Aira Force.

The path is 20m above the lake and unfortunately there is no clear route down to the lake itself through the bracken. Occupy yourself with spotting the different tree species (which include beech, sycamore, willow, rowan and juniper) until you get to Silver Point. This is a distinct promontory and if you divert to the tip you get an excellent view north and south, along Ullswater.

The path undulates with a steep uphill pull now and again. For the most part you feel completely isolated. The fell side rises above you on the left, from time to time covered in mixed woodland. Depending on the time of day you set off, you are usually well into the walk before you begin encountering fellow walkers who are doing the route from the Howtown direction. If you get tired of saying hello, bear in mind that it could be worse; you could have been doing the same route and be stuck behind them all (a particular problem when everyone piles off the steamer at Howtown and queues to go through the kissing gate at the start of the walk).

You eventually drop down through the woods to approach a dry stone wall and Scalehow Beck. The path curves around the corner of the field boundary and you drop down to cross the beck via a wooden footbridge. The route continues on the other side but it is worth diverting upstream to find Scalehow Force, an attractive waterfall in the trees.

From the footbridge, continue along the main path. You now have fields and the stone wall between the path and the lake though there are still good views to the lake. Keep to the wall and the path

Ullswater *(Bill Stainton)*

brings you down to Sandwick, a tiny hamlet. When you reach the tarmac road, turn left, go past Bushey Cottage and Beckside Farm, and follow the lane through the wooden farm gate and over the wooden vehicle bridge. The lane becomes a track which leads you through the field to another farm gate. Our route goes right here (signed 'Public Footpath'), off the track and along the dry stone wall, past a ruined building. According to a local farmer I met, this pile of stones was once a ferryman's cottage. I gather the farmer didn't value it too highly as a site of great historical interest; he was busy recycling the stones for the upkeep of his walls.

The path takes you through another gate and across an open field, with a lovely view ahead of the tree-lined lake shore. Through two more gates and the path rejoins the lake shore. Keep to the wall and another gate leads you into Hallinhag Wood, a delightful mixed woodland which runs right down to the shore line.

The wood lies on the flanks of Hallin Fell and as you round the hillside and leave the wood behind, you can see the northern end of Ullswater. The distinctive cone at Pooley Bridge is Dunmallard Hill, the site of an Iron Age hill fort and Pooley Bridges first settlement.

The path now begins to drop you gently towards the shore and you overlook Howtown Wyke ('wyke' is the local name for bay).

Keep your eyes open for the steamers coming into the pier; from the south they pass right below your viewpoint [4]. A bench seat is thoughtfully provided.

Setting off again, you pass the edge of a field boundary and the garden to Waternook House and drop down to a kissing gate. Down the steps and a made path brings you back along the lake shore. Follow the shore round to the small wood and at the footbridge go left to the pier.

Alternatively, if you keep going straight you come to the road. Turn right and five minutes walk brings you to the Howtown Hotel, which does teas and has a public bar for walkers at the rear of the hotel. Don't get too settled, though – keep an eye on the steamer timetable!

NOTES

[1] Patterdale – St Patrick's Valley – is named after the 6th-century saint who brought Christianity to the area. St Patrick's church is a Victorian building.

[2] Ullswater is named after another of the ubiquitous Norse settlers, in this case Lulph, the first Lord of Ullswater. The lake is one of four in the Lake District designated a public highway the others are Derwent Water, Coniston Water and Windermere. Speed restrictions imposed by the National Park Authority in 1983 keep the lake clear of power boats and water skiers. The lake is 12km (7.5 miles) long, 1.2km (0.75 miles) wide, and 62.4m (205ft) at its deepest point.

[3] Lyulph's Tower is another reference to the first Lord of Ullswater, although in this case the connection is rather more distant; the tower was built as a hunting lodge in the 1800s by the Duke of Norfolk.

[4] The Ullswater Navigation and Transit Company Limited began running boats on Ullswater in 1855. The present two craft are over a hundred years old: Lady of the Lake was launched in 1877 and Raven in 1889. They were originally steam driven but were converted to diesel in the 1930s. The journey from Howtown to Glenridding takes about 35 minutes and if it is blowing a gale, each launch has a welcoming bar below decks.

23

CRUMMOCK WATER

This is a terrific walk which takes in a variety of spectacular views, including Criffel and the Solway Firth. Crummock Water is long and peaceful and has distinct atmosphere all of its own. You can make a complete circuit of the lake but the eastern shore is rather spoilt for walkers by he presence of the B5289. The western shore is wilder, more isolated and this route gives you the opportunity to visit Scale Force, the Lake District's longest waterfall.

Distance and terrain: 10.5km (6.5 miles). Level walking along the shore of Crummock Water with a long slow climb to Scale Force and the back of Mellbreak. A gentle descent. Good underfoot but may be wet, especially around the pumping station.

Parking: Lanthwaite Wood, National Trust pay-and-display car park (GR 149215), one mile east of Loweswater village.

The start of this walk is ideal. You spurn the road and head off immediately into Lanthwaite Wood. Leave the car park via the wooden gate (opposite end to the entrance) and follow the forestry track through the trees. You're accompanied on your right by the sound of water from Cocker Beck [1].

Ignore the waymarked path which goes off left (a rather energetic route up Whiteside) and continue straight along the track, passing two more forks left (one of which has a barrier across). This brings you to the shingle beach at the foot of Crummock Water[2] and an excellent view of Mellbreak. This is an atmospheric spot, dominated by a tall Scots pine, with a tremendous sweeping view of the lake and surrounding fells.

The path forks here. Go right and you immediately encounter the concrete dam wall and the weir. Cross over the two footbridges,

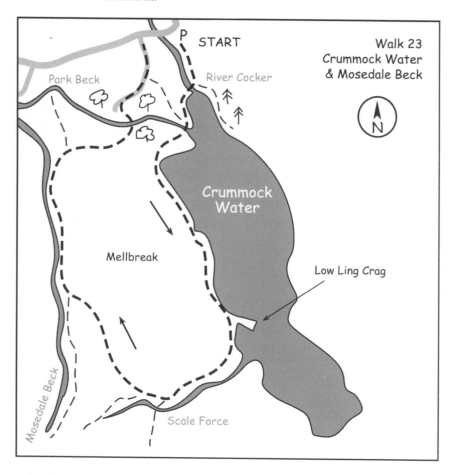

which span the weir. The second bridge feels very precarious, heightened by the tremendous rush of water passing underneath.

Once on the other side of the river, you have a lovely walk long the edge of the lake, through a small wood, with terrific views of Mellbreak, Whiteside and the lower flanks of Grasmoor.

The path runs alongside the concrete dam wall, crosses Park Beck and then arrives at the pumping station, built by Workington Corporation in 1903. Continue along the edge of the dam; depending on recent weather, you may have to walk along the top of the dam to avoid the waterlogged marsh on your right. Fortunately the lake is only a couple of feet deep at this point, so it is not too intimidating.

Crummock Water and, from left: Rannerdale Knotts, High Crag, High Stile and Red Pike
(Bill Stainton)

The wall ends at a wooden fence. Cross the stile and continue through the field, keeping to the shore.

The path climbs above the level of the lake, past hawthorn, birch and rowan. The conical fell you can see on the far shore is Rannerdale Knotts and just beyond it is the gloriously named High Snockrigg. The sharp, triangular peak to the left of Rannerdale is Whiteless Pike.

The views get better and better. The path leads you across a shingle shore, through a kissing gate and out of the field via a stile (note the dog hole alongside, very thoughtful). You now have a lovely, bracken-covered field on your right, sweeping up the lower flanks of Mellbreak. There are a number of fast flowing becks coming down Mellbreak but the extraordinary thing is how few of them you have to cross; most of them just soak into the ground. This makes the ground very marshy in winter, so you may feel like climbing higher, or sticking closer to the shore, to avoid washing off too much wax from your boots.

After a mile of steady walking along the shore line you approach a very impressive crag on your right and can see the odd-shaped peninsula of Low Ling Crag. This is a real post-Ice Age oddity – a 'roche moutonnée', to give its proper term. Divert down to stand at the end and take in the tremendous all-round views.

From the crag, continue along the shore another 200m or so and the path begins to head inland. You cross a couple of smaller becks then arrive at Scale Beck. Head right and follow the beck upstream, without crossing the wooden footbridge. You climb to a wire fence and walk between the fence and the river, climbing to a wooden footbridge. In theory, we should cross the stile here and head up the fell, along the old bridleway to Ennerdale. But this would involve missing Scale Force, so at the expense of a little tricky navigation later on, continue uphill, beside the river. In fact at this point you are walking between two rivers, formed by a rocky moraine.

After 100m you can see the waterfall, just visible in the patch of trees ahead and to your left. As you join the fence line again, go left across the wooden footbridge and go the few metres upstream to Scale Force.

This is a very picturesque spot. The 52m (172ft) waterfall plummets through a narrow cleft in the rock face, surrounded by a copse of trees. It is a double cascade and with care you can walk into the cleft, right up to the lower cascade. (In fact, if conditions are right, you can climb to the foot of the upper cascade, but I'm not about to recommend it.) Emerging from the cleft, you are faced with an expansive view across Crummock Water to Whiteless, Grasmoor and Whiteside.

Go back to the footbridge. The route we want to follow goes up along the fence line, to climb the back of Mellbreak. There isn't a distinct footpath, although there is a stile half way along the fence. If conditions are right, go to the corner of the fence, cross the beck and climb alongside the fence. Alternatively, if it is very boggy, bear left and curve round as soon as you can to rejoin the fence higher up. There are a number of paths which make things a little confusing. Stay in sight of the fence and you are going in the right general direction.

The 155m-high summit of Mellbreak is fenced because the fell is in private ownership. Many regard fencing in a Lakeland peak as highly controversial, although there area few stiles provided to cross it. As you climb, you can look back to Crummock Water and beyond that to the road from Newlands Valley as it drops down to Buttermere.

At the top of the fenced boundary, another fence comes in from the left. Go through the gate and straight ahead, over a boggy section at the back of Mellbreak. You now lose the views to Crummock and this wide, open moorland is very windswept and isolated. The path leads straight across the marsh to a mystery metal gate. The fence here has long since gone, so actually going through the gate would be obsessive. Instead pause and look north east to see Criffel and the Solway Firth. It is also worth keeping your eyes open for kestrels along this section of the walk.

From the mystery gate, the path gently descends a pleasant green fell side, heading towards the distant river. Crossing a couple of smaller becks, you eventually arrive at another fence line, between you and Mosedale Beck. Follow the track downhill and see how much you can remember from school geography lessons about oxbow bends; Mosedale Beck has some good examples. This valley was once mined for lead there is an old mine shaft on the far side of the valley. The last mine closed in the 1890s.

Passing a small cairn and an old stone wall, you come to at what appears to be a brick water tank. Just above this on the fell side is a deep hole, which I like to think is probably a boggart den [3]. This is a nice, easy descent which gives you plenty of opportunity to take in the views. The route eventually forks at the apex of a triangular plantation of fir. Left is the main track, which would bring you down at Loweswater village. However, we've still interesting things to explore, so take the path right, past the pines, keeping to the fence line. You get a good view of the end of Mellbreak this way, a towering crag which looms on your right. You may also get a glimpse of Loweswater and the village through the trees on your left and a view of Whiteless ahead of you.

When you pass through the stone wall, there is a better view of Loweswater. Don't leave doing this walk too long after publication date, however, as the view is due to be interrupted by the spruce plantation on the other side of the wall. For the time being they're all young enough not to get in the way.

This is a very pretty, sheltered section of the walk. The path drops to Green Wood, an ancient sessile oak woodland. At the corner of the stone wall, the path does loop, which brings you left, back to the bottom of the wall land a wooden farm gate. As you make the loop, you get a glimpse of Whiteless and Crummock Water.

Go through the gate and along the narrow track between the walls. This all feels very unexplored along here. Keep to the track and it takes you between a group of houses to a T-junction with a tarmac lane.

According to the wonderfully optimistic Ordinance Survey there is a right of way which goes across the fields and back to the lake shore path from this point. Unless you happen to be wearing waders, I do not recommend it. Instead, go left, over the road bridge over Park Beck and along to the next T-junction. Go right and along the quiet country lane, enjoying yet more views of Whiteless.

The lane curves left past Muncaster House to bring you to a cross-roads. Go right, over the bridge and you are back at the entrance of Lanthwaite Wood car park.

NOTES

[1] Cocker Beck flows from Crummock Water across Lorton Vale to Cockermouth, where it joins the River Derwent and flows out to sea at Workington, on the west coast.

[2] Crummock Water is a Celtic name, appropriate for a lake which is so strongly reminiscent of a Scottish loch. The name means the bent or curved lake. Crummock Water is 4km (2.5 miles) long and less than 1km (0.6 mile) wide. At the deepest point it is 44m (144ft). The lake is owned by the National Trust.

[3] The boggart is a very rare Lakeland beast, comprising half fox and half badger. There are two varieties; one has the front half of a fox and the back half of a badger, the other the reverse. Sightings are very rare and you usually only see the back half as the animal disappears over a wall. If you don't believe me, a fine example is exhibited in a glass case in the Twa Dogs Inn, Keswick.

24

DERWENT WATER

Known to many as the Queen of the Lakes, Derwent Water offers magnificent opportunities for waterside walking. There is a route which completely circles the lake and is for the most part right on the lake shore. Add superb mountain scenery, delightful woodland and the opportunity to catch a lake launch if you get tired and you have a recipe for a classic walk.

Distance and terrain: The complete circuit of the lake is 16km (10 miles). The walk described below omits the final section from Hawes End to Keswick and is 11km (6.9 miles). Level walking throughout.

Parking: Pay-and-display car park at Keswick boat landings.

To give the best views, I have taken a clockwise route around the lake and split the walk into sections, based on the jetty points for the Derwent Water launches. This means that if you get tired, or simply do not fancy the entire route, you can break the walk with a boat trip.

I haven't included the final section of the circuit, from Hawes End back to Keswick; it involves road walking and for the most part is away from the lake shore. If you insist on completing the circuit, it is not difficult to follow from the map. For the rest of us, give it a miss and catch the launch back from Hawes End. I won't tell a soul.

KESWICK BOAT LANDINGS TO ASHNESS GATE

Two choices from the car park. If you are feeling antisocial or have dogs, children or grannies straining to be let off the leash, there is a gate at the far corner of the car park which takes you through the woods and joins the walk at Strandshag Bay.

Alternatively, leave the car park and walk along the lane past the

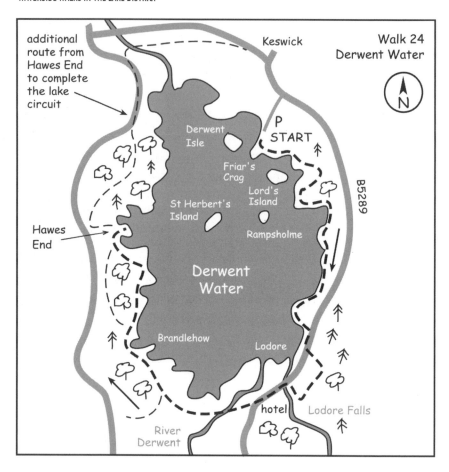

boat landings and the National Trust information centre. This is part of the walk which is popular with Sunday afternoon strollers. As you leave the tarmac and walk through the woods to Friars Crag, it is not hard to see why it draws so many people. Go past the slate memorial to Ruskin [1], and right to the end of the peninsula for a brilliant view of the lake and the mountains of Borrowdale. You can have a rest on the second best positioned bench seat in the Lake District.

On the path to Friars Crag, you will pass a memorial to Canon Hardwicke Rawnsley, one of the three founders of the National Trust. The crag was purchased by the Trust in 1922.

Continue around the wooded knoll, through a gate and follow the

Derwent Water with Friars Crag in the background *(Bill Stainton)*

path along the shore, through a field. As you approach the wood ahead of you, a path comes in from the left from the car park. If you see anyone clutching this book, be sure to tell them what they missed.

The path leads you through mixed woodland, with glimpses of Castlehead, the wooded hill on your left. There is a rich variety of trees in this boggy wood. Look out for Scots pine, oak, yew, beech and alder. It is also a mass of bluebells in the spring.

You emerge from the wood and join a track, skirting around a field. Turn right and the track goes past a house (signed 'National Trust Stable Hills Cottage'). Just as you come in sight of a white bungalow, a path goes off to the left (signed 'National Trust Footpath'). The path follows the lake shore with a view of the lake and islands [2] as good as anything from Friars Crag.

A gate takes you onto another wooded peninsula. The path goes left but a diversion straight takes you to another seat and view. As you walk back to the path, look on the shore to your right and you will see a large, split boulder. Go and investigate [3].

The path now drops to the pebbled beach and continues along the edge o the lake. This is a terrific part of the route which takes you

Nearby Ashness Bridge *(Norman Buckley)*

through an impressive stand of Scots pines. On a good summer day, you can have fun trying to count the tiny figures climbing the ridge of Cat Bells, on the opposite side of the lake. Just before you reach the wooden footbridge, look on the right and you can find a holly which is practically growing out of a Scots pine.

After the footbridge, you come to a rock outcrop. This is a short scramble and I leave you to pick the best route. Once on the top, you are 6m above the lake and walking parallel to the road, which is just the other side of the stone wall. Take care with dogs and children. The path narrows along here. Unless you want to walk along the road, follow the path as far as you can and take the first opportunity to drop down to the shore. Continue along the beach to the launch pier at Ashness Gate.

ASHNESS GATE TO LODORE LANDING

Continue past the pier, over a stile and along a pleasant, grassy stretch of shore line. You are skirting around Barrow Bay at this point and as you come to a footbridge, look north for a lovely view towards Skiddaw. As you walk along the far side of the bay, you can see along the shore to the Swiss Lodore Hotel and, beyond that, to Castle Crag, standing in the Jaws of Borrowdale.

Over another stile and along a built up section of path and you come to the National Trust Kettlewell car park. If you want to catch the launch at the Lodore landing stage, you need to continue along the road for 200m or so. Alternatively, cross the road and go through the gap in the wall, opposite the car park entrance, into Strutta Wood. Follow the path along the fence line to a small gate. Go through and bear right, walking below ancient scree to another gate. Ignore the path left and go through the gate, continuing parallel to the road to another path (signed 'Permitted Path avoiding Road').

This path takes you around a field boundary. Where the path splits, a marker indicates that you should go right. Alternatively if you go left, you come to Lodore Falls [4].

Go back downstream to rejoin the path and over a narrow bridge to the back of the Lodore Swiss Hotel. (Or the Stakis Hotel as it is now called, though for me it will always be remembered as the Swiss Lodore.) As you reach the drive to the hotel, look out for the honesty box in the back wall of the building. If you have diverted to see the waterfall, put 5p into the box. Then continue to the road and turn left. Note the toilet block on your right. It's the last one you will see until you arrive back at Keswick.

LODORE LANDING TO BRANDLEHOW

120m along the road brings you to a gate and narrow stile, signed 'Public Footpath to Manesty'. This next section of the walk is across the flat flood plain at the head of Derwent Water. You are surrounded by mountains, with a good view along the lake to Skiddaw. You cross the River Derwent via an elegantly arched, 30m footbridge and then set off across 300m of board walk across the reeds. Note the passing places thoughtfully provided. This board walk is narrow and can be slippery in winter. The terrific view will probably draw all your attention and it is hard to stop falling off the boards. Past a wooded knoll, through a gate and over more boards to the lake shore again, to walk around Great Bay.

Just beyond an old stone wall, the path splits. Continue straight to cross another three sets of board walks and then the path splits again. Go right and you walk around two wooded knolls, right along the lake shore. Just around the second knoll, there is a small, rocky peninsula and what I submit is the best-sited bench in the Lake District [5]. Beat that for a view!

Continue along the shore to cross a stile and enter Manesty Woods. The path leads you through the woods and around Abbots Bay. Look out for Otter Island, the tiny, wooded island in the centre of the bay.

The path brings you to a tarmac track. Go right, past the stone bungalow (signed 'National Trust Footpath to Brandlehow') and look out for the slate picnic table in the wood on your right. At the fork in the track, turn left and along the rough track to Brandlehow Bay.

The path goes right, past Brandlehow house and along the shore. This is a strange section of the shore, the woods standing on old mine workings. Depending on the recent rainfall, you can keep to the shore all the way round to the landing stage at Brandlehow, in the edge of the woods. If the lake is high, go left at the wire fence, uphill to a kissing gate. Then follow the path straight through the woods to the landing stage.

BRANDLEHOW TO HAWES END

There is a choice of route at this point. A higher footpath leads through the Brandlehow Park to Hawes End but leaves the lake shore to do this. This is a good walk, with plenty of features of interest. It makes a good walk in its own right, if you catch the launch to Brandlehow [6]. The rickety-looking pier at Brandlehow is an exciting landing point.

However, I recommend keeping to the shore line wherever possible, so, from the landing stage, follow the lower footpath through Brandlehow Woods. The next section of the route is a delightful, 1km stroll through lovely mixed woodland. After winding around a couple of small bays, you come to the landing stage at Old Brandlehow. The path forks here. Go left, along the edge of the woods. The field here gets very wet in winter. That's a walkway along the edge of the field, not a massive park bench.

The path leads to a fence. Go through the gate and keep right through the field to the Hawes End landing stage. This is a very pretty spot, an ideal place to investigate the rucksack for any remaining sandwiches whilst you wait for the launch back to Keswick [7].

NOTES

[1] Ruskin is the philosophical father of the National Trust and the slate memorial commemorates his connections with the Lake District. It bears an inscription which reads:

The first thing I remember
As an event in my life was being
taken by my nurse to the brow of
Friars Crag on Derwentwater

[2] Derwent Water has four major islands. The nearest to the shore at this point is Lords Island, once the home of the Earl of Derwent Water, hence the name. The most interesting island is back towards the boat landings, Derwent Isle. It was originally called Vicars Island but, in 1778, was bought by an eccentric individual called Joseph Pocklington. He built a house on the island and then deciding to improve the view by constructing a set of follies, including a Druids' temple and a stone circle. Guide book writers of the time referred to it as Pocklington's Island but were sceptical about the follies; William Gell called them 'an awkward jumble of fantastic gew gaws'.

The other two islands are Rampsholme and St Herbert's Island. The latter was the hermitage of St Herbert, the close friend and disciple of St Cuthbert. It was a place of pilgrimage in the seventh century and the embarkation point for monks making the trip to the island was the rocky peninsula south of the boat landings, which is why it is now known as Friars Crag.

There are a number of much smaller islands, plus a local oddity known as Floating Island. This is a mass of water plants and vegetation which surfaces in Great Bay, usually around mid-October, buoyed up by marsh gases.

[3] The inside of this split boulder, 1m in diameter, has been carefully carved and polished. It is an unobtrusive sculpture created and placed here to commemorate the centenary of the National Trust in 1995. It is a beautiful piece of work with strong Celtic resonance. It looks like the rock was simply sliced open to reveal the sculpture inside. In the current climate of X-Files mania, I wonder how many passers-by think that all the rocks around here contain similar weird fossil remains.

[4] This is a spectacular 27m (90ft) cataract in a rocky ravine, surrounded by trees. A real bonus on the walk. Very popular with the Victorians who constructed a turnstile to admit visitors. They also kept a small cannon at the hotel and for 20p would fire a blank shot to demonstrate the echo. The waterfall is on land owned by the hotel, hence the honesty box.

[5] Derwent Water is 4.8km (3 miles) long, 1.6km (1.25 miles) wide and around 22m (72ft) at its deepest point. It is an important area for wildlife conservation with rare fish species, extensive wetlands and important habitats for wildfowl. The lake and River Derwent were given special protected status in spring 1997 when they were designated a Site of Special Scientific Interest. Many experts regard Borrowdale as one of Northern Europe's most important examples of a big valley ecosystem.

[6] Brandlehow Park was the first property purchased by the National Trust in 1902, just seven years after the Trust was formed. It cost £6500.

[7] See Appendix 2 for details of the KeswickLlaunch service.

THE COAST

Crossing Cartmell Sands, Morecambe Bay, from Ulverston to Flookburgh *(Bill Stainton)*

25

MORECAMBE BAY

Not so much a Waterside Walk as walking through water – and salt water at that. This is a unique walk, with a fascinating perspective on the Lakeland fells. It is also unusual in that it should only be done accompanied by the official Sands Guide and for this reason I do not offer a route description. I must emphasise that it is extremely dangerous to attempt even part of this walk without the guide. The Bay has numerous quicksands and their positions shift daily.

Not long ago, the local papers reported a particularly lucky rescue: A man had strolled out onto the sands one evening and nearly drowned, trapped in the quicksand for several hours as the tide rushed in. He was very lucky; by the time the rescue party dug him out, the sea water was lapping at his neck.

If this sounds frightening – it is meant to. People have died on the sands within shouting distance of the shore. However, go with the official guide and you will be perfectly safe. For dates and further details, see Appendix 2.

Distance and terrain: About 13km (8 miles). Completely flat. Some wading to be undertaken so shorts and sandals are recommended. Most people do the walk in bare feet. The weather can change quickly out on the Bay, so take warm and windproof layers and a small rucksack to carry your shoes. The walk takes about three hours.

Parking: Requires meticulous planning and careful co-ordination or a friend with a second car. Park at Kents Bank or Grange-over-Sands and take the train to the start of the walk, or park in Arnside and jump on the train when it is over.

Superb, unique, exhilarating and something to tell your friends about when you get home. Guided walks are led across the Morecambe Bay sands by the official guide [1], Cedric Robinson. At the time of writing, the starting point is outside the Albion Hotel, Arnside. You won't be able to miss the start; just look for crowds of

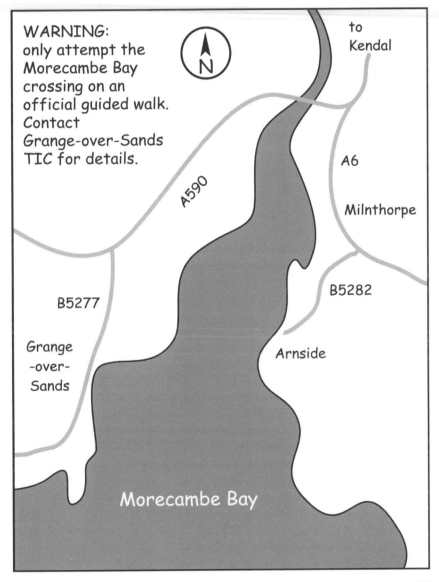

WARNING: only attempt the Morecambe Bay crossing on an official guided walk. Contact Grange-over-Sands TIC for details.

N

to Kendal

A6

A590

Milnthorpe

B5277

B5282

Grange -over- Sands

Arnside

Morecambe Bay

people chatting excitedly and wearing odd combinations of fleeces, mountain jackets and sandals. There are often charity groups undertaking the walk, with somebody collecting money before the start. There is also the opportunity to make a donation and buy an official certificate at the end of the walk.

Note that charity groups sometimes book the whole walk – to check that there is space available, contact Grange-over-Sands tourist information centre (see Appendix 2) or ring the Guide direct.

The exact route varies according to the conditions out on the Bay. A considerable amount of preparation and experience goes into making sure the walk is safe and enjoyable on the day. In particular, the channel of the River Kent can alter dramatically and the Guide and his assistants mark the route beforehand, planting bushes – known as 'brobs' – to show where it is safe to cross. (Last time we walked it, my chief researcher thought the brobs were for an entirely different purpose and proceeded to lift a leg at each one he encountered. All the other dogs on the walk promptly followed suit.)

Once out on the sands, you are in a completely different world. Apart from the other people on the walk, it is isolated and wild. Seagulls wheel overhead and you may spot the occasional fisherman, out on a tractor, preparing nets. The view of the Lakeland fells is particularly striking [2].

Once you reach the Kent channel, the walk halts. Cedric and his team check that it is safe to cross and then distribute the group along the channel. The crossing itself can be very exciting, sometimes wading thigh deep through the strong rush of water, children racing each other to the other side. Depending on the exact route taken, you may cross the channel two or three times during the course of the walk.

By the time you reach the far side, you will be exhausted but exhilarated. There is usually a scramble for the loos at Kents Bank, not least to wash mud off your feet. Don't forget to get your signed certificate.

NOTES

[1]   The first Guide to the Sands was appointed in 1326 by the Abbot of Furness, although it is possible local monks funded an unofficial guide earlier than this. After the dissolution of the monasteries by Henry VIII in 1548, the Guide was appointed by the Duchy of Lancaster. It

Sunset from Arnside *(Bill Stainton)*

was the Guides duty to pilot coaches across the Bay, meeting them at Hest Bank, near Lancaster, and marking out the route with branches of laurel, a practise which continues today. The coming of the Furness railway in 1857 almost put an end to the route but recreational crossing began to become popular in 1936, after the publication of a series of local newspaper articles. The walks ceased during the second World War, resuming in 1947. Cedric Robinson was appointed official Guide in the Letters Patent under the seals of the Duchy of Lancaster and the County Palatine in October 1963. He lives at the Guides Cottage and is a member of H.M. Coastguard.

[2] Morecambe Bay was a major route into the Lake District at the time of the Romans. In 1322, Robert the Bruce led his army across the Bay and into north Lancashire. As the popularity of the Lakes grew as a tourist destination, coaches began to drive across the Bay, many passengers preferring it to the rough, dusty roads particularly after the introduction of a toll road at Levens Bridge, just south of Kendal. Early coaches were far too heavy and often got bogged down in the sand. The first purpose-built public conveyance was introduced in 1781, a diligence or light coach, which could carry three people. The

WATERSIDE WALKS IN THE LAKE DISTRICT

coach company's advertising assured customers that they had '... procured a sober and careful driver who is well acquainted with the sands, and humbly hope that their plan will meet with due encouragement as this is the most cheap, safe and expeditious method of crossing the sands to and from Ulverston'. The coach trip from Lancaster took around two hours and cost five shillings.

APPENDIX 1

MORE WATERSIDE WALKS

Here are ten suggestions for additional walks, beginning with a round-up of the remaining six lakes:

BASSENTHWAITE LAKE

There are several good, shorter walks on the eastern shore, particularly around Mirehouse. Park at Dodd Wood car park, walk to the lake shore via St Bega's church and combine with a visit to Mirehouse (check opening times for Mirehouse by calling Keswick information centre).

The National Park Authority owns Bassenthwaite Lake and has developed a number of walks along the western and northern shores. Look out for the information boards in the lay-bys.

ENNERDALE WATER

There is a good 11km (7.75 miles) circuit of the lake. Park at Bowness Knott and head off clockwise around the lake. Forest Enterprise has also laid out a Nine Becks walk through the woods. Leaflets usually available in the car park.

WAST WATER

An excellent circular 12.25km (8.5 miles) shore walk. Start at the National Trust car park at the head of Wast Water and go clockwise around the lake. Don't be put off by the long stretch along the road, it is very quiet and you can amuse yourself spotting the National Park logo, formed by the mountains at the head of the lake. The walk along the screes on the eastern shore is particularly exciting and there's an attractive footpath through Low Wood.

ESTHWAITE WATER

Unfortunately the shore line is private with only one short stretch of public access at the northern end of this quiet, pretty lake.

WINDERMERE

England's largest lake but curiously frustrating from the point of view of waterside walking. Several shorter walks can be made at various access points, notably Cockshott Point, in Bowness, and at Wray Castle, on the north east shore. For a longer route, catch a Windermere lake cruiser to Lakeside and walk back along the south-western shore to Ferry Nab. Catch the car ferry and walk back to Bowness via Cockshott Point.

HAWESWATER

Over the past few years, the National Park Authority has developed an excellent circular walk around the lake. This route is quiet all year round and ideal for hardy, energetic types who want to get right away from it all. Magnificent scenery. Car parking is rarely a problem unless the lake level has dropped during a hot summer and the remains of Mardale village have become visible.

* * *

Finally, here is a short selection of favourites around tarns, rivers and waterfalls:

ALCOCK TARN, GRASMERE

A strenuous but rewarding walk which climbs the side of Rydal Fell to a small, isolated tarn. Continuing the route over Butter Crags and down via Greenhead Gill gives a good tour of Wordsworth country. Walk back via the river side path through Grasmere village.

WYTHBURN, THIRLMERE

A pleasant walk from Steel End farm, Thirlmere, walking up the eastern bank of the river to the footbridge and down the western. Good views of Thirlmere as you get towards the head of the valley.

LANGSTRATH, BORROWDALE

A 9.5km (6 miles) walk in spectacular mountain country, in the heart of Borrowdale. Begin at Stonethwaite, just south of Rosthwaite, and follow the eastern bank of Langstrath Beck, past Gallen Force. Cross via the footbridge at the confluence of Langstrath Beck and Stake Beck and back along the lane.

RIVER DUDDON

Several smaller walks along various parts of the Duddon. Worth seeking out to enjoy the most peaceful of the major Lakeland dales.

BROTHERS WATER

Park at Cow Bridge, Hartsop, just off the A592, then walk anticlockwise around the tarn. You begin by following Dovedale Beck, an extremely pretty river. The footpath continues over the fields to Sykeside Farm, crosses the road and then heads back down to Hartsop via a footpath just off the road. As you approach the tarn again, there is a permitted footpath between the road and the tarn. Good views on the way back down but it's a pity that the road is so close. But for that, the walk would have been one of the main routes in the book.

APPENDIX 2

VISITOR ATTRACTIONS AND PUBLIC TRANSPORT

This section takes each of the 25 waterside walks in turn and lists local visitor attractions and public transport information. There are a great many visitor attractions in the Lakes, with new ones opening each year. This section gives a run down of the more established attractions within striking distance of each walk. Armed with this information you have no excuse for heading back to your hotel as soon as the walk is finished.

WALK 1 – SPOUT FORCE

VISITOR ATTRACTIONS

Whinlatter Forest Park, Whinlatter, Nr Keswick. Telephone 017687 78469. An excellent visitor centre 3.5km (2.2 miles) back along the road towards Keswick. Features interactive exhibitions, displays and an excellent café.

WALK 2 – THE HOWK

VISITOR ATTRACTIONS

Priests Mill, Caldbeck, Nr Penrith. Telephone 016974 78369. A very carefully converted former water mill, now the home of an excellent café, bookshop, jewellery craft shop and a number of other attractions.

WALK 3 – STOCKGHYLL

VISITOR ATTRACTIONS

The Bridge House, on Rydal Road, features in postcard racks throughout the area. It's a tiny house over a stream and is now a National Trust information centre.

Adrian Sankey's Glass House, Rydal Road, Ambleside. Telephone 015394 37346. Just behind the Bridge House. An imaginative development of glass workshop and a splendid café and restaurant.

Armitt Museum, Rydal Road, Ambleside. Telephone 015394 31212. Paintings, photographs and rare books connected with the area, plus Beatrix Potter's original botanical paintings.

Homes of Football, Lake Road, Ambleside. Telephone 015394 34440. Everything you needed to know about football but didn't expect to find in Ambleside. An excellent photographic exhibition.

WALK 4 – AIRA FORCE

VISITOR ATTRACTIONS

For attractions, see the Ullswater walk.

WALK 5 – MILL BECK

VISITOR ATTRACTIONS

See the River Greta walk.

WALK 6 – FINSTHWAITE TARN

VISITOR ATTRACTIONS

Stott Park Bobbin Mill, Finsthwaite, Newby Bridge. Telephone 015395 31087. See route description for details.

Lakeside and Haverthwaite Railway, Newby Bridge. Telephone 015395 31594. A restored section of the Lakeside to Ulverston line, run by enthusiasts with steam trains connecting Haverthwaite to the boat services at Lakeside.

WALK 7 – LANTY'S TARN

VISITOR ATTRACTIONS

See Ullswater

WALK 8 – TARN HOWS

VISITOR ATTRACTIONS

Beatrix Potter Gallery, Main Street, Hawkshead. Telephone 015394 35355. A small museum in the old solicitors offices which belonged to William Heelis, Beatrix Potter's husband. The exhibition tells the story of Beatrix Potter herself, rather than her books, and includes her exquisite plant paintings.

Hill Top, Near Sawrey, Windermere. Telephone 015394 36269. Beatrix Potter's famous Lake District home, a place of pilgrimage for fans from all over the world.

See the Levers Water entry for attractions in Coniston.

WALK 9 – STANLEY GILL & RIVER ESK

VISITOR ATTRACTIONS

Eskdale Corn Mill, Boot, Eskdale. Telephone 019467 23335. A converted corn mill, no longer working but a good display on the history and technology.

Muncaster Castle, Muncaster, Ravenglass. Telephone 01229 717203. Originally a pele tower, now a large mansion set in magnificent grounds overlooking the Esk estuary. Famous for rhododendrons and azaleas and as the centre for the British Owl Trust.

Ravenglass & Eskdale Railway, Ravenglass. Telephone 01229 717171. La'al Ratty to the locals, this narrow gauge railway was once a mining line but is now run for the benefit of passengers. Not only a useful service but a brilliant attraction in its own right.

WALK 10 – RIVER GRETA

VISITOR ATTRACTIONS

Keswick Museum and Art Gallery, Fitz Park, Keswick. Telephone 017687 73263. One of Cumbria's oldest museums, full of oddities. Contains a collection of original manuscripts from Southey and the Lake poets and features a small art gallery.

Cumberland Pencil Museum, Southey Works, Keswick. Telephone 017687 73626. The history of pencil making, from the discovery of graphite in the fells of Borrowdale to the world's largest pencil, a Guinness Record-holder. Good fun for children of all ages.

Cars of the Stars Museum, Standish Street, Keswick. Telephone 017687 73757. A museum which appeals to car and film buffs alike. Contains original vehicles from films and TV series such as Chitty, Chitty, Bang, Bang, James Bond, Batman, Knight Rider and Back to the Future.

The Puzzling Place, Museum Square, Keswick. Telephone 017687 75102. Around 80 puzzles and brain teasers on display in a privately run museum. The Calvert Trust, Old Windebrowe, Keswick. Telephone 017687 72112.

Provides riding and outdoor facilities for the disabled. The Calvert Trust can be also be contacted at their headquarters at Little Crosthwaite, Under Skiddaw. Telephone 017687 72254.

WALK 11 – RIVER DERWENT

VISITOR ATTRACTIONS

See River Greta for attractions in Keswick

WALK 12 – EASEDALE TARN

VISITOR ATTRACTIONS

Heaton Cooper Studio, Grasmere. Telephone 015394 35280. Small gallery selling cards and framed prints of paintings by William Heaton Cooper, to many the classic painter of Lakeland landscapes.

See Rydal Water and Grasmere walk for further attractions.

WALK 13 – LEVERS WATER & CHURCH BECK

VISITOR ATTRACTIONS

Ruskin Museum, The Institute, Yewdale Road, Coniston. Telephone 015394 411164. Museum devoted to Ruskin, including correspondence, possessions and his geology collection. Also features displays about Donald Campbell and Arthur Ransome.

Brantwood, Coniston. Telephone 015394 41396. Ruskin's home, open to the public in accordance with his wishes. Excellent nature trail around the grounds, special exhibitions and an excellent café.

See Coniston Water for details of the Gondola, Coniston Boating Centre and the Coniston Launches.

WALK 14 – RIVER LOWTHER

VISITOR ATTRACTIONS

Lakeland Bird of Prey Centre, Lowther Park, Hackthorpe, Penrith. Telephone 01931 712746. A breeding and training centre for falcons, with displays all year.

WALK 15 – TAYLORGILL FORCE & SPRINKLING TARN
VISITOR ATTRACTIONS
See River Greta or Loweswater.

WALK 16 – CONISTON WATER
VISITOR ATTRACTIONS
Coniston Launches, Castle Buildings, Near Sawrey, Ambleside. Telephone 015394 36216. Regular launch service on the lake.

Gondola Steam Launch, Coniston. Telephone 015394 63850. The best way to see the lake, travelling in Victorian splendour. Note that sailings are restricted to good weather. To check that the Gondola is running, ring the Coniston tourist information centre (see Appendix 3).

Coniston Boating Centre, Lake Road, Coniston. Telephone 015394 41366.Run by the National Park Authority, the centre offers launching facilities and boat storage. It also hires out dinghies, rowing boats, canoes and environmentally-friendly, electric powered motor boats. Café on site.

For details of the Ruskin Museum and Brantwood, see Walk 13.

WALK 17 – BUTTERMERE
VISITOR ATTRACTIONS
See River Greta details for the nearest visitor attractions.

WALK 18 – LOWESWATER
VISITOR ATTRACTIONS
Loweswater village is not exactly packed with visitor attractions, but Cockermouth is only a few miles north and offers the following:

Wordsworth House, Main Street, Cockermouth. Telephone 01900 824805.The birthplace of William and Dorothy Wordsworth. A fine Georgian mansion with a splendid garden. Owned by the National Trust.

The Printing Museum, 102 Main Street, Cockermouth. Telephone 01900 824984. A small, privately run collection of old printing blocks and machines, tucked round the back of Winkworth's second-hand bookshop.

Toy and Model Museum, Banks Court, Market Place, Cockermouth. Telephone 01900 827606. An award-winning museum exhibiting a wide range of toys from 1900 to the present with a visitor-operated tinplate model railway.

Jennings Brewery – Castle Brewery, Cockermouth. Telephone 01900 821011. Tours of the brewery and a good shop on site. A must for aficionados of real ale.

Lakeland Sheep & Wool Centre, Egremont Road, Cockermouth. Telephone 01900 822673. Slightly bonkers visitor centre devoted to the Lake District's major inhabitant. Includes a live sheep show. I am not making any of this up, go and see for yourself.

For those of you who want the ultimate in picturesque accommodation: **Holme Wood Bothay**. Contact National Trust Enterprises on 015394 35599.

WALK 19 – THIRLMERE

VISITOR ATTRACTIONS

Nearest visitor attractions are in Grasmere or Keswick.

WALK 20 – RYDAL WATER AND GRASMERE

VISITOR ATTRACTIONS

Dove Cottage, Town End, Grasmere. Telephone 015394 35544. William Wordsworth's most famous home, where he lived whilst at the height of his powers as a poet. Almost all the furniture belonged to Wordsworth and the house and garden have been restored to how they were in Wordsworth's day. There are guided tours of the house and an excellent museum. Restaurant on site.

Rydal Mount, Rydal, Near Ambleside. Telephone 015394 33002. Wordsworth's final home; he died here in 1850. Very attractive grounds and a view which has hardly changed since he lived here.

WALK 21 – ELTERWATER

VISITOR ATTRACTIONS

The nearest visitor attractions as such are in Grasmere or Ambleside. **The Britannia Inn**, however, is very picturesque and well worth looking into (purely out of interest in vernacular architecture, of course).

WALK 22 – ULLSWATER

Ullswater Navigation and Transit Company, Glenridding Pier, Glenridding, Ullswater. Telephone 017684 82229.

VISITOR ATTRACTIONS

Dalemain, Penrith. Telephone 017684 86450. Large, Georgian-fronted house with interesting architecture and family history. Fascinating gardens and a superb tea shop in the baronial hall.

WALK 23 – CRUMMOCK WATER

VISITOR ATTRACTIONS

See Loweswater for details.

WALK 24 – DERWENT WATER

Derwent Water Launch Company, Lake Side, Keswick. Telephone 017687 72263. Runs throughout the year, daily except Christmas Day.

VISITOR ATTRACTIONS

Worth popping into the **Theatre by the Lake** (telephone 017687 74411) to see what is on. This is a very imaginative development on the site of the old Blue Box touring theatre. Three plays run during the summer holidays, alternating to give visitors the chance to see all three during a fortnight stay in the area. For further Keswick attractions, see River Greta details.

WALK 25 – MORECAMBE BAY

Buses to **Grange-over-Sands** from Windermere and Kendal are available during the week but less frequent during the weekend. If you can get to Kendal, you can make a protracted rail trek via Lancaster.

Regular rail links between Grange-over-Sands and Arnside, check well in advance to make sure you tie in with the walk. Telephone British Rail on 0345 484950. Grange-over-Sands tourist information centre also has train times, specifically for the walk. Ring the TIC on 015395 34026.

VISITOR ATTRACTIONS

Holker Hall, Cark-in-Cartmel, Grange-over-Sands. Telephone 015395 58328. A superb stately home dating back to the 17th century, owned by the Cavendish family. Extensively developed over the past fifteen years, there is always a lot going on at Holker. Special events include hot air ballooning, vintage car rallies (it is also the home of the Lakeland Motor Museum) and bird of prey demonstrations. Pick up a leaflet at Grange TIC and if you want the place more to yourself, come back and explore the magnificent house and the gardens during the week. Very keen to cater for families, there is a children's playground and a cafeteria on site.

APPENDIX 3

GENERAL TOURIST INFORMATION

In this section you will find general information about the area, including tourist information centres, National Park organisations and, most important, the weather service number for the Lake District.

PUBLIC TRANSPORT

There is no need to feel a second class citizen in the Lakes just because you do not use a car. Even if you have access to a car, there is something invigorating about leaving it at home for the day and doing a walk via public transport. You feel very smug afterwards. However, please bear in mind that in the brave new world of deregulation, bus routes can come and go with alarming swiftness. For up-to-date information, use the Traveline information service operated by Cumbria County Council, telephone 0870 608 2608 or visit www.traveline.org.uk and ask for their 'To & Through The Lakes', a free leaflet which has a handy map of bus and boat routes in Cumbria.

One welcome development in recent years has been the involvement of the National Trust, which runs a bus service in Borrowdale during the summer, telephone 015394 35599. The main bus company is Stagecoach, which has worked hard to link up routes – see their Lakeland Explorer leaflet (available from tourist information centres).

THE LAKE DISTRICT NATIONAL PARK

The Lake District is the largest of 12 national parks in England and Wales, covering an area of 885 square miles. It was created in 1951 and is administered by the Lake District National Park Authority (NPA), a statutory body which receives most of its funding from government and local councils. Very little of the land within the Park is owned by the NPA; unlike national parks in the United States and other European countries, the countryside within the Park boundary is privately owned.

The statutory aims of the NPA are to conserve the natural beauty, wildlife and cultural heritage of the Lake District, to promote opportunities for enjoyment and understanding of the national park and to foster the interests of the local community. The NPA operates as one of the planning authorities for the area and is also heavily involved in maintenance, countryside access and promotion of the area through its information and visitor centres. It also produces a range of publications about the area, which you can find in any of its information centres (see below).

You are most likely to encounter the NPA through its information centres or by bumping into one of its Rangers. These individuals patrol the Park, working on footpath maintenance, liaise with farmers over access, offering advice and policing the by-laws. They are supported by around 350 Voluntary Wardens, who give their time to work with the NPA.

The Lake District National Park Authority runs public events and activities throughout the year, from working days with a ranger to children's picnics at Brockhole. These are all listed in the Events booklet, available from information centres. To contact the National Park headquarters, write to:

Lake District National Park Authority, Murley Moss, Oxenholme Road, Kendal, Cumbria LA9 7RL. www.lake-district.gov.uk

NATIONAL PARK VISITOR CENTRE

The NPA runs the National Park Visitor Centre at Brockhole, Windermere. This is an ex-mansion house on the shore of Windermere with extensive grounds and lovely gardens. You can catch a boat to Brockhole from Waterhead or Bowness and picnic in the grounds, making it a good waterside potter in its own right. Brockhole is home to a range of events throughout the season and is also a good source of general information about the Lakes. Open daily, April to November, admission free (although there is a parking charge).

National Park Visitor Centre, Brockhole, Windermere, Cumbria LA23 1LJ. Telephone 015394 46601

THE NATIONAL TRUST

The National Trust should not to be confused with the National Park. Both were formed to care for and conserve the countryside, promote enjoyment of the area and both run information centres and have rangers (though the NT calls them wardens). However the National Trust is a registered charity, receiving its money from donations and from income generated from its properties. Also, unlike the National Park Authority, it owns all the land it cares for, which, in the case of the Lake District, is around a quarter of the area within the National Park boundary.

The National Trust for Places of Historic Interest or Natural Beauty, to give it its full title, has strong historic links with the Lake District. The ideas which formed the basis for the movement were propounded by the writer and philosopher John Ruskin in the late nineteenth century. Indeed, it was the climate of opinion generated by opposition to the Thirlmere reservoir (see the Thirlmere and Harrop Tarn walk) which fostered the birth of the Trust. The Trust was officially registered on 12 January 1895 and one of its three founder members was Canon Hardwicke Rawnsley, vicar of Crosthwaite and Canon of Carlisle. The Trusts first property was Brandlehow Woods, acquired in 1902 (see the Derwent Water walk).

The Trust has a number of famous houses in the Lake District, including Townend, a wonderful statesman farmers house in Troutbeck, near Windermere, and Hill Top, Beatrix Potter's home at Near Sawrey. For a full list of properties and information centres in the Lake District, contact:

The National Trust, North West Regional Office, The Hollens, Grasmere, Cumbria LA22 9QZ. Telephone 015394 35599. www.nationaltrust.org.uk

TOURIST INFORMATION CENTRES

There are TICs in all towns and most major villages in Cumbria. They vary from small corner shops which give out local information, to large, networked TICs which can book you into accommodation on the other side of the country. The centres run by the Lake District National Park Authority are particularly useful for walking advice and information and often have excellent exhibitions and a range of publications specifically about the National Park.

LAKE DISTRICT NATIONAL PARK INFORMATION CENTRES

Bowness-on-Windermere	015394 42895	closed winter
Broughton-in-Furness	01229 716115	
Coniston	015394 41533	closed winter
Glenridding	017684 82414	closed winter
Grasmere	015394 35245	closed winter
Hawkshead	015394 36525	closed winter
Keswick Moot Hall	017687 72645	
Pooley Bridge	017684 86530	closed winter
Seatoller	017687 77294	closed winter
Waterhead, Ambleside	015394 32729	closed winter

Broughton-in-Furness is run jointly by the National Park Authority and South Lakeland District Council and is open all year.

Not all of the National Park centres are networked, which means they will not offer accommodation booking beyond their immediate area.

In addition, there are twelve Local Information Points (LIPs), where National Park information is available in local shops and post offices, mostly in the outlying areas of the Lake District. These can be a good source of information about the immediate locality but they are not geared up to answer telephone queries:

Brampton Post Office, Brampton Grange, Shap

Barn Door Shop, Wasdale Head

Boot Post Office, Boot, Eskdale

Maple Tree Corner Shop, Elterwater

Ennerdale Bridge Post Office, Ennerdale, near Cleator Moor

Far Sawrey Post Office, near Hawkshead

Forest Spinners, Rusland, Haverthwaite

Gosforth Pottery, Gosforth, near Seascale

High Lorton Post Office, Lorton Vale, near Cockermouth

Ravenglass Station Booking Office, Ravenglass & Eskdale Railway, Ravenglass

St Bees Post Office, 122 Main Street, St Bees

Ulpha Post Office, Duddon Valley, near Broughton-in-Furness

OTHER TOURIST INFORMATION CENTRES IN CUMBRIA

Unless stated otherwise, these are all open throughout the year. As part of the networked service, they offer accommodation booking and many also operate a bureau de change.

Alston	01434 382244	closed winter
Ambleside	015394 32582	
Appleby	017683 51177	
Barrow-in-Furness	01229 894784	
Brampton	016977 3433	closed winter
Carlisle	01228 625600	
Cockermouth	01900 822634	
Egremont	01946 820693	
Grange-over-Sands	015395 34026	
Kendal	01539 725758	
Killington Lake	015396 20138	
Kirkby Stephen	017683 71199	
Longtown	01228 792835	
Maryport	01900 813738	
Penrith	01768 867466	
Sedbergh	015396 20125	
Silloth-on-Solway	016973 31944	
Southwaite	016974 73445/6	
Ulverston	01229 587120	
Whitehaven	01946 32729	
Windermere	015394 46499	
Workington	01900 606699	

The TICs are run by a variety of local authorities, many of which publish their own accommodation guides to the area. These list registered guest houses, hotels, camp sites and caravan sites, with contact details and lists of facilities. Contact the nearest TIC to the part of the Lakes you are planning to visit.

CUMBRIA TOURIST BOARD

Another source of useful information and accommodation details, particularly on Cumbria as a whole. Contact them prior to your visit by writing to:

Cumbria Tourist Board, Ashleigh, Holly Road, Windermere, Cumbria LA23 2AQ.

Telephone 015394 44444. www.gocumbria.co.uk

OTHER ORGANISATIONS

There are a number of other organisations which work to conserve and protect the Lake District. These are for the committed Lakeland enthusiast. If you care about the area or are feeling guilty about the amount of Lake District soil you scrape off your boots when you get home, you may want to get involved.

BRITISH TRUST FOR CONSERVATION VOLUNTEERS

The BTCV is Britain's largest practical conservation charity, with over 85,000 volunteers. Anyone can join and help work in a wide range of conservation activities, from building a dry stone wall and footpath maintenance, to forestry and studying wildlife. The BTCV runs day, weekend and week long conservation holidays, called Natural Breaks and volunteers come from all sections of the community. It is probably the most practical way you can get involved in caring for the Lake District. For more details of their work or a copy of their Natural Breaks holidays, contact:

British Trust for Conservation Volunteers, National Park Centre, Brockhole, Windermere, Cumbria LA23 1LJ. Telephone 015394 43098. www.btcv.org

FRIENDS OF THE LAKE DISTRICT

A very worthwhile association which operates as a pressure group to promote and organise concerted action for the protection and conservation of the Lake District. It is very influential and has run a number of very successful campaigns in the past. It also represents the Campaign to Protect Rural England (CPRE) and you don't have to live in the area to become a member.

Friends of the Lake District, Murley Moss, Oxenholme Road, Kendal, Cumbria LA9 7NF. Telephone 01539 720788 www.fld.org.uk

MOUNTAIN RESCUE PROCEDURE

In the event of serious trouble on the fells, you may need to call out the mountain rescue service. There are a number of teams operating in Cumbria. If a member of your group is hurt, at least one person should stay with the injured party whilst one preferably two other person make their way to the nearest telephone. Dial 999 and ask for the police. They will then call out the appropriate team. If you can, provide an accurate OS grid reference to give the location of the injured person.

Do not call up the mountain rescue on your mobile phone if you are just a bit lost or feeling tired. Members of the mountain rescue teams are volunteers and a call out will often mean leaving their jobs for many hours. It is a service for emergencies.

LAKE DISTRICT WEATHERLINE

The National Park operates a weather forecasting service, supplied direct by the Newcastle Met Office and always more accurate than the national forecasts. Available 24 hours a day and updated twice daily. In winter, it includes fell-top conditions supplied by the National Park rangers.

Weatherline telephone: 017687 75757.

OTHER USEFUL CUMBRIAN WEBSITES

These give a variety of general information, plus links and webcams:
www.thecumbriadirectory.com
www.cumbria-online.co.uk
www.bbc.co.uk/cumbria
www.thisisthelakedistrict.co.uk

Also of interest:

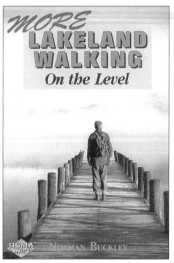

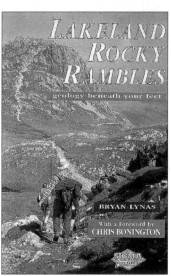

LAKELAND WALKING: On the Level
Norman Buckley
Walk among the highest mountains of Lakeland and avoid the steep ascents - with no compromises on the views! "A good spread of walks" - RAMBLING TODAY. £6.95

MORE LAKELAND WALKING: On the Level
Norman Buckley
"...a wide selection of circular walks demanding minimum effort and providing maximum enjoyment." - THE KESWICK REMINDER £6.95

LAKELAND CHURCH WALKS
Peter Donaghy and John Laidler
Nominated for Lakeland Book of The Year, 2002 – and with a foreword by Simon Jenkins of *The Times* – here is a collection of 30 detailed circular walks from 3½ to 12 miles with alternative shorter options, each starting from a noteworthy church. Easy-to-follow instructions combined with cross-referenced maps make these walks ideal both for those who wish to complete the full walk or those who prefer to visit the church and have a short stroll. £8.95

LAKELAND ROCKY RAMBLES: Geology beneath your feet
Bryan Lynas
This book by science-writer and geologist Bryan Lynas, is introduced by Chris Bonington, who conquered Everest and many other mountains and who now lives in the Lake District. It's both a guide to carefully-selected Lake District rambles and a detailed explanation of the rocks and scenery that you'll actually see, walk on or scramble over. This is real hands-on (or feet-on!) science in Nature's own laboratory where you can touch the exhibits. £9.95

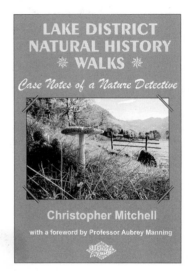

LAKE DISTRICT NATURAL HISTORY WALKS

Christopher Mitchell

Discover the Lake District's hidden wildlife, geology and archaeology - familiar landscapes in a new light. With 18 walks to choose from, readers can become nature detectives and solve the hidden mysteries. Detailed maps, clear drawings and photographs complement the text. £7.95

WALKS IN ANCIENT LAKELAND

Robert Harris

Enjoy a 'Walk in Ancient Lakeland' and discover sites and monuments from the Neolithic and Bronze Ages you never knew existed. Discover the great stone circles, standing stones and burial cairns which still decorate these beautiful hills. Follow the ancient trackways linking these ancient sites and explore largely unknown areas to uncover the mysteries of the lives of our ancestors in this timeless landscape. £7.95

IN SEARCH OF SWALLOWS & AMAZONS

Roger Wardale

As featured on BBC Radio 4! Three decades of Ransome hunting with text and photographs to identify the locations of the ever-popular series of books. There's a two-fold pleasure in this book: enjoying the original stories and discovering the farms, rivers, islands, towns and hills that formed their backdrop. 'Recommended reading' – *The Daily Telegraph* £8.95

COME BACK TO EDEN: Lakeland's Northern Neighbour

John Hurst

"Its leisurely and affectionate narrative and its vintage photographs remind us that the history of a nation is shaped not only by kings and politicians but also by ordinary mnd and women" – George Bott, *The Keswick Reminder*